YOUTH AND WORK IN AUSTRALIA

Comprehensive Policy Agenda

ORGANISATION FOR ECONOMIC CO-OPERATION AND DEVELOPMENT

Ministry of Education, Ontario
Information Centre, 13th Floor,
Mowat Block, Queen's Park,
Toronto, Ont.   M7A 1L2

Pursuant to article 1 of the Convention signed in Paris on 14th December, 1960, and which came into force on 30th September, 1961, the Organisation for Economic Co-operation and Development (OECD) shall promote policies designed:

- to achieve the highest sustainable economic growth and employment and a rising standard of living in Member countries, while maintaining financial stability, and thus to contribute to the development of the world economy;
- to contribute to sound economic expansion in Member as well as non-member countries in the process of economic development; and
- to contribute to the expansion of world trade on a multilateral, non-discriminatory basis in accordance with international obligations.

The Signatories of the Convention on the OECD are Austria, Belgium, Canada, Denmark, France, the Federal Republic of Germany, Greece, Iceland, Ireland, Italy, Luxembourg, the Netherlands, Norway, Portugal, Spain, Sweden, Switzerland, Turkey, the United Kingdom and the United States. The following countries acceded subsequently to this Convention (the dates are those on which the instruments of accession were deposited): Japan (28th April, 1964), Finland (28th January, 1969), Australia (7th June, 1971) and New Zealand (29th May, 1973).

The Socialist Federal Republic of Yugoslavia takes part in certain work of the OECD (agreement of 28th October, 1961).

Publié en français sous le titre :

LES JEUNES ET L'EMPLOI
EN AUSTRALIE

© OECD, 1986
Application for permission to reproduce or translate
all or part of this publication should be made to:
Head of Publications Service, OECD
2, rue André-Pascal, 75775 PARIS CEDEX 16, France.

This report is one of a series of analytical studies and country reviews examining employment and unemployment, and youth policies in OECD countries.

It examines the employment situation facing young people in Australia and, by drawing in part on the experience of other OECD countries, suggests new policy initiatives or changes in existing education, training, labour market and income support policies, which would improve long-term employment prospects for today's youth. The report pays special attention to the changes in these policies that are necessitated by structural adjustments in the Australian economy.

This volume is published on the responsibility of the Secretary-General, but the views expressed are those of the examiners and do not commit the Organisation or the national authorities concerned.

The examiners' report is followed by a summary of the discussions of a meeting between the examiners, the Australian delegation and representatives from other OECD countries.

Also available

NEW POLICIES FOR THE YOUNG (August 1985)
(81 85 03 1) ISBN 92-64-12705-4 116 pages   £6.50   US$13.00   F65.00

"CERI" (Centre for Educational Research and Innovation)

THE EDUCATION OF THE HANDICAPPED ADOLESCENT: HANDICAPPED YOUTH AT WORK. Personal Experiences of School-leavers (July 1985)
(96 85 02 1) ISBN 92-64-12708-9 84 pages   £5.50   US$11.00   F55.00

BECOMING ADULT IN A CHANGING SOCIETY by James S. Coleman and Torsten Husén (July 1985)
(96 85 01 1) ISBN 92-64-12709-7 82 pages   £5.00   US$10.00   F50.00

YOUTH EMPLOYMENT IN FRANCE. Recent Strategies (November 1984)
(81 84 09 1) ISBN 92-64-12629-5 112 pages   £4.50   US$9.00   F45.00

THE NATURE OF YOUTH UNEMPLOYMENT. An Analysis for Policy-makers (July 1984)
(81 84 07 1) ISBN 92-64-12573-6 224 pages   £9.50   US$19.00   F95.00

IMPROVING YOUTH EMPLOYMENT OPPORTUNITIES. Policies for Ireland and Portugal (February 1984)
(81 84 01 1) ISBN 92-64-12537-X 174 pages   £7.00   US$14.00   F70.00

YOUTH WITHOUT WORK. Three Countries Approach the Problem. *Report by Shirley Williams and other Experts* (September 1981)
(81 81 02 1) ISBN 92-64-12240-0 256 pages   £6.80   US$15.00   F68.00

YOUTH UNEMPLOYMENT. The Causes and Consequences (December 1980)
(81 80 05 1) ISBN 92-64-12137-4 136 pages   £3.20   US$8.00   F32.00

YOUTH UNEMPLOYMENT:
Volume I: General Report (October 1978)
(81 78 04 1) ISBN 92-64-11815-2 140 pages   £4.90   US$10.00   F40.00

Volume II: Inventory of Measures Concerning the Employment and Unemployment of Young People (October 1978)
(81 78 02 1) ISBN 92-64-11806-3 184 pages   £4.20   US$8.50   F34.00

Prices charged at the OECD Publications Office.

THE OECD CATALOGUE OF PUBLICATIONS *and supplements will be sent free of charge on request addressed either to OECD Publications Office, 2, rue André-Pascal, 75775 PARIS CEDEX 16, or to the OECD Sales Agent in your country.*

TABLE OF CONTENTS

The OECD Examiners and the Australian Delegation 6

Part One

THE EXAMINERS' REPORT

Foreword	. . . .	9
Chapter 1.	Summary of Findings and Recommendations	10
Chapter 2.	Employment and Unemployment	14
Chapter 3.	Education and Training	28
Chapter 4.	Income Support	53
Chapter 5.	An Entitlement for Young People	67
Chapter 6.	Rationalising and Decentralising Governance Arrangements	75
Chapter 7.	A Framework for New Initiatives	80
Bibliography	. . . .	87

Part Two

RECORD OF THE REVIEW MEETING
Paris, 28th March 1985

Theme I.	An Entitlement and Alternative Employment Opportunities for Young People	94
Theme II.	Employment and Unemployment	96
Theme III.	Education and Training	98
Theme IV.	Income Support	100
Annex :	Terms of Reference of the OECD Review of Youth Policies in Australia	102

THE OECD EXAMINERS

Mrs. Ritt Bjerregaard, Chairman — Member of Parliament, Denmark
Former Minister of Education, and
Former Minister of Social Affairs

Mrs. Anke Fuchs — Member of Parliament,
Federal Republic of Germany
Former Minister of Health, Youth and Family Affairs

Sir Richard O'Brien — Chairman, Engineering Industry Training Board, United Kingdom
Former Chairman of the Manpower Services Commission

The examiners were assisted by

Mr. Gregory Wurzburg — OECD Secretariat

THE AUSTRALIAN DELEGATION

Mr. J.S. Dawkins — Minister Assisting the Prime Minister in Youth Affairs
Office of the Prime Minister
Canberra, ACT

Mr. Alan Mawer — Consultant to the Minister in Youth Affairs
Canberra, ACT

Mr. Alan Abrahart — Office of Youth Affairs
Canberra, ACT

Mr. Fred Argy — Ambassador to the OECD

Mr. Geoff McAlpine — Counsellor
Permanent Delegation to the OECD

Part One

THE EXAMINERS' REPORT

FOREWORD

In early 1983, shortly after the elections brought the current Labour Government to power, the Australian authorities invited the OECD to assemble a team of experts to advise the government on the youth unemployment situation and ways for dealing with it. It was hoped that a team with international experience might have some fresh views on assessing the relative seriousness of the problems facing young people, making new uses of resources for better meeting those problems, and suggesting new interventions, outgrowths, perhaps, of schemes that have worked in other OECD countries.

This report of the OECD examiners is based on information, evidence and opinions gleaned from an extensive background report prepared by the Australian authorities, and additional public and private reports, publications, and news accounts. The most important information came from the two-and-a-half-week visit by the examiners to Australia in November and December 1983. During their visit, they held nearly sixty meetings and interviews with more than four hundred persons, including young people; local, state, and Commonwealth officials; youth workers; parents; politicians; teachers; employers; and trade union members.

In conducting the review, the examiners necessarily have been selective. In the time available it was possible to visit only a few cities and towns in New South Wales, Queensland, South Australia, Victoria, and the Capital Territory. The examiners focused on those topics where an outside perspective would complement the views of experts in Australia, and where an outside view representing no vested interests would have a high degree of credibility. The report presents the examiners' views on what they think are the most important problems facing young people in Australia. In considering remedies, they have tried to shed light on issues that require ordering priorities, straddle departmental lines, or pit the interests of groups or institutions against one another. The overall objective of the report is to take a broad view of the elements of the situation affecting large numbers of young people and put them into perspective relative to one another, and in a limited sense, relative to interests in Australia that extend beyond the youth employment situation.

This report offers a rough outline of new youth policies in Australia. It is hardly a blueprint or detailed specification for new programmes. That will only come out of the give-and-take of public debate among Australians. It is hoped, however, that outside views on what constitute the most serious problems facing young people, and what constitute the most important remedies will broaden and maybe even enrich that debate.

The examiners would like to express their gratitude to the Australian Commonwealth authorities for their co-operation and courtesy in collecting and providing information they needed to carry out their work, answering questions, and making the necessary arrangements for their visit to Australia. The examiners are particularly grateful for the background report prepared under Commonwealth direction in advance of their visit. *Youth Policies Programmes and Issues: An Australian Background Paper* [available from the Commonwealth Publishing Service, Canberra, ACT] is a useful update on the situation of young people in Australia and review of government policies on their behalf.

Ritt Bjerregaard

Chapter 1

SUMMARY OF FINDINGS AND RECOMMENDATIONS

Australia faces two problems in the mid-1980s with regard to its young people: *i)* high rates of unemployment and underemployment; and *ii)* low levels of educational attainment and occupational skills and unequal access to the education and training opportunities that exist. These two problems, their causes and consequences, are discussed below. Remedies are suggested in three areas: employment, education and training, and income support. The rationale for and details of these are discussed in the chapters that follow.

The first problem, that of unemployment and underemployment among young people, is the more acute. (By "young people", the examiners refer to 16 to 24 year-old persons unless otherwise indicated.) It poses an immediate economic hardship for young people and, for some, their families as well; it is postponing adulthood and economic independence; it is wasting human resources. While unemployment and underemployment are so widespread they affect virtually all groups of young people, they fall especially heavily on girls and young women, and disadvantaged youth, reinforcing past patterns of socio-economic inequality in the labour market by shutting off opportunities for progress.

The first problem has also attracted the most public attention. Unemployment in general, and youth unemployment in particular, figured prominently as issues in the national elections in March 1983 and December 1984. But it is not just the magnitude and intensity of youth unemployment and underemployment that is such a concern now. The problem is a shock to past expectations that a person's opportunities were limited only by one's competence, ambitions and willingness to work.

This problem of unemployment and underemployment is of course a direct consequence of the last decade of high inflation and slow economic growth that Australia has suffered through with the rest of the OECD countries. But youth unemployment and underemployment are a product of more than overall economic conditions, and they require more than an upswing in economic growth to cure them. This is where the second problem is relevant.

Not only has the aggregate employment growth been too slow to absorb all the young people entering the labour force over the last several years, but the structure of net growth has changed. The service sector is growing, and with that growth there has been proportionately greater growth in part-time employment. But there has also been growth in high-technology occupations and jobs that are dependent in one way or another on computer technology. On the other hand, excessive protection of certain domestic industries notwithstanding, Australia is witnessing a decline, like that witnessed in other industrialised countries, in some sectors of the economy, manufacturing in particular, where there is heavy reliance on unskilled and semi-skilled workers. The end product of these shifts in the structure of the economy is a greater demand for a more highly trained workforce than Australia has had in the past.

Between now and the end of the century, if Australia shares the expected experience of the other OECD countries, its economy will require an increasingly better educated and trained workforce. There will be little opportunity for would-be workers with low levels of education and no occupational skills, or only out-of-date skills. Those developments are likely to put a strain on the current education and training arrangements.

Presently those arrangements are geared to meeting the needs of an economy requiring mostly skilled and semi-skilled labour. Although the arrangements for secondary and tertiary education, and technical and trade training provide a fairly broad mix of competences, the proportions are wrong. Most people enter the labour force with less than twelve years of education and no specific occupational skill. There is a need to assure a higher minimum level of preparation for working life (and adulthood) as well as a need to increase the proportion with technical skills.

Beside the overall needs of the economy for educational competences and occupational skills, there is a need to assure an equitable distribution of those competences and skills. Under the present arrangements, females are poorly served. Their classroom preparation and the guidance and counselling they receive in secondary education do not equip them for the education or training they need to enter higher-paying, higher-status, and traditionally male jobs. Similarly, preparation, guidance and counselling in higher education, in apprenticeship and institution-based training fail to break down the usual patterns of occupational segregation by sex.

Economically disadvantaged youths also need to be served better. Under the current income support arrangements, arrangements that are an integral part of the education and training opportunities offered, young people who need to maximise their income in the short term find the greatest reward in looking for work or taking unemployment benefits. They are more likely to forego those education and training activities that would produce substantial gains over the long term, because the short-term economic benefits of participating in education and training are so low relative to unemployment or wages.

Without substantial changes in the education and training arrangements, and the income support measures to permit participation in education and training, socio-economic equality will suffer. Those who fare most poorly in the labour market will continue to be the most poorly served. As educational and occupational skills become more important to success in the labour force, these deficiencies will aggravate socio-economic inequality. Without substantial changes in the education and training arrangements, the Australian economy may suffer, lacking the qualified manpower needed to grow and compete in an international economy.

Generally, there is a need to raise the minimum level of competences and preparation of young people when they finish compulsory education. There is a need to assure that all young people are guaranteed an opportunity for education or training beyond the lower secondary level, for those who want it, and adequate preparation for work and adulthood, for those who do not continue. To accomplish this, the authorities should establish a "Youth Entitlement" for those continuing secondary education through year twelve, entering apprenticeship, enrolling in further education or vocational training. The "Youth Entitlement" should better articulate the relationship among education and training institutions and also assure that when young people leave those institutions they have the necessary preparation for entering the labour market and working. Authorities should also establish an Entitlement Year for those not going on to education and training, guaranteeing the opportunity to receive adequate job search, life skills training, orientation to the world of work and a credential indicating to employers that they are job-ready.

In developing and carrying out comprehensive policies for youth, Commonwealth authorities should recognise the need to rationalise responsibilities not only at the Commonwealth level, but among the three levels of government – Commonwealth, state and local – and among other players such as employers and unions. In this rationalisation process, the Commonwealth should exercise its national leadership role to ensure that decisions affecting provision of services are made as closely as possible to the level at which those services are provided. Additionally, the Commonwealth should ensure that it provides the kind of informational, evaluative, and other technical assistance that can be developed and disseminated most effectively and efficiently on a centralised basis.

The level of resources that the Australian authorities decide to allocate to supporting youth policies is a political issue. For that reason, the examiners make no specific recommendations on resource levels though they do provide some cost estimates for information purposes. They are of the opinion, however, that relative to other OECD countries, Australia can indeed afford to do more for its young people.

The current youth unemployment and underemployment problem has acted as an alarm, bringing attention not only to the immediate problem young people face in the labour market, but to the more far-reaching concerns with education and training. This alarm has given added impetus to efforts that have already been underway to improve education and training arrangements. In a narrow sense, this collateral concern with education and training arrangements is misdirected: no matter how good those arrangements might be, Australia would still have high youth unemployment rates today. But in a larger sense, it is absolutely right. Changes are needed to improve the prospects for young people entering the labour market several years from now, and to improve the opportunities for today's young people as they grow older.

The examiners have placed the greatest emphasis on a long-term view of needs of young people as well as of the Australian economy. Their main reason for doing this is to counteract short-term political pressures. Unless the long-term concerns with education and training are highlighted, they risk being overshadowed by the short-term concerns with high unemployment and underemployment for youth. The latter is a problem with immediate and visible impacts but it is a problem whose solution is largely independent of long-term changes in education and training arrangements. In fact, both problems need to be dealt with. The examiners felt, however, that problems with education and training arrangements needed extra attention in order to receive the priority treatment they deserve.

The examiners concentrate on education and training also because of the difficulty of establishing a national agenda in those areas, involving Commonwealth, state, local and community responsibilities, and progress is likely to depend on negotiation and consensus-building which, in turn, are likely to require as much encouragement as possible.

This report deals with policies affecting young people in general. It does not deal with particular issues regarding Aboriginal and migrant youth because the examiners concluded that the review could not cover those issues effectively. On the basis of limited observations, the examiners believe that young Aboriginals and migrants in Australia suffer particular problems with regard to geographical and cultural isolation, language and discrimination. These are problems that compound the difficulties these young people share with other Australians regarding employment, education, training and poverty. These are problems that are likely to require specialised policies over and above general youth policies. The examiners encourage the Australian authorities to continue to assure that Aboriginal and migrant youth are served by the programmes serving other young people. But the authorities should also monitor those programmes to determine whether Aboriginal and migrant youth are participating in them and whether additional measures are needed to meet their needs.

The examiners' findings and recommendations are presented in the following chapters. Chapter 2 examines the employment situation facing young people, and suggests what needs to be done with respect to labour market policies to improve these prospects. Chapter 3 analyses the education and training arrangements and suggests how they might be changed. Chapter 4 deals with income support. The examiners view income support arrangements as a subordinate issue most relevant to the needs of young people in the role they play in facilitating participation in education and training. In Chapter 5, they suggest how education, training, employment, and income-support arrangements might be combined in an "Entitlement" to better assure that all young people have at least some basic preparation for work and adulthood. Chapter 6 considers the difficulties of fashioning a "national policy" in a federal system. Chapter 7 suggests an overall framework in which to consider its recommendations, and establishes priorities.

Throughout the report the examiners present the rationale for their conclusions and recommendations. Readers wanting more detail on conditions and arrangements in Australia should consult the bibliography, and refer to *Youth Policies, Programmes and Issues: An Australian Background Paper.*

As to matters of definition, "Commonwealth" means federal; "youth" and "young people" refer to those who are 15 to 24 years old; "teenagers" to those who are 15 to 19; and "young adults" to those who are 20 to 24 years old.

Chapter 2

EMPLOYMENT AND UNEMPLOYMENT

Unemployment among young people has been the galvanising force behind the current government's mandate for a reordering of youth policies in Australia. The consensus in Australia is that, even with recent declines in the unemployment rate, the level of joblessness is still intolerably high and that new policies are needed to bring down youth unemployment. But in focusing on the immediate high levels of youth unemployment there is a danger of overlooking shifts in the nature of youth employment. In the process of formulating youth policies, these shifts in youth employment need to be accounted for as much as the immediate problem of unemployment, or the short-term measures to get young people back to work may do nothing to correct conditions that breed long-term labour market problems for some, permanently isolating them from the economic mainstream.

The Labour Market Situation

Unemployment

The youth unemployment situation has created shock waves in Australia partly because of the scale of the problem, but also because of the speed with which it has deteriorated. While youth unemployment in the OECD area rose steadily after the 1979 oil shock, in Australia it stayed at the plateau of just under 12.5 per cent that it reached following the first oil shock until 1981 when it declined to 10.8 per cent; that was more than a quarter below the rate for the OECD area. But between 1981 and 1983, youth unemployment jumped by nearly two-thirds, from 10.8 to 17.9 per cent; it reached 22.6 per cent for teenagers in August 1983. In that time, labour force participation rates dropped only slightly, but youth employment dropped by 8 per cent and full-time employment for teenagers plunged 20 per cent. Since then, however, improvements in the general economic climate have brought overall youth unemployment down to 16.1 per cent for 1984; the OECD expects a further decline below 16 per cent[1].

There is a combination of factors contributing to high youth unemployment in Australia, but the most important explanation for its sharp increase in 1982 and the current high level is general macro-economic conditions. The post-oil-shock recession that hit most OECD countries in 1980 and early 1981 did not hit the Australian economy until mid-1982. But then a set of related factors – an inflationary surge, high real interest rates, decreased competitiveness in international markets combined with high demand for imports, upward pressures on wage costs, and weakened profitability – undermined demand. The overall unemployment rate rose by a fourth to 6.9 per cent from 1981 to 1982[2].

Though the burden of unemployment has fallen most heavily on young people, the principal effect at the margin apparently has not been to increase the duration of unemployment, but to increase the frequency of unemployment spells. The mean and medium duration of unemployment for teenagers has increased, but not as much as it has for most older workers.

The economic recovery that got under way in Australia in 1984 is not likely to benefit young people as much as others because of growing segmentation in Australian labour markets (these trends are discussed later in the chapter). Additionally, unemployment rates for females most likely underestimate the true extent of joblessness among them, and consequently the number of jobs required to put them back to work. This is especially true for teenage girls. Since the late 1960s their labour force participation rates have tended to fluctuate by greater and greater amounts in response to changes in the economy. With economic downturns, they have been more likely than boys to withdraw from the labour force. The exception was between 1982 and 1983 when boys were especially hard hit by the decline in manufacturing and apprenticeship positions. Participation rates for boys dropped then by four points, while they actually edged up a point for girls. But the number of discouraged girls out of the labour force is likely to be high. In September 1982, as the delayed effects of the 1979 oil shock hit Australia, the number of discouraged females of all ages outnumbered discouraged males by more than seven to one. No figures are available on the number of discouraged teenage females who withdrew from the labour force, but evidence would indicate that the number is much higher than for males, and the number of teenage girls who would seek employment when jobs are available is considerably larger than the measured unemployment rate would imply. Even if an economic recovery does create many more jobs for young people, the sheer size of the unemployed population now will require years to be reduced significantly. By one calculation, the net job deficit that has to be made up in order to get teenage unemployment down to levels preceding those of the past decade of stagflation, is more than 140 000 jobs[3]. If young people were to keep their share of the labour force, this would require more than 1.3 million additional jobs in Australia[4]. It is obviously going to require more than a strong economic recovery to get Australia's young people back to work in the foreseeable future.

Underemployment and Labour Market Segmentation

While youth unemployment is serious in Australia, the *employment* problems are also cause for worry. For some young people who find work, their jobs are more likely than before to be marginal. The jobs are not well paid and appear to be of limited value for further mobility. More and more, young people are working part-time instead of full-time, and are working in sectors of the economy that are declining or offer little long-term opportunity for career (and income) growth. The situation is worse for girls and young women.

The most dramatic change in youth employment patterns has been the shift from full-time to part-time employment (see Tables 1 and 2). Between 1970 and 1983, when total youth employment grew by only 2.5 per cent, and teenage employment actually dropped, part-time employment of young people grew by more than 25 per cent, a rate that was nearly three times as fast as the increase in part-time employment among adults. The incidence of part-time work for young women increased from 12 to 15 per cent, at a rate that was three times the rate for young men. The incidence of part-time employment among teenage girls nearly quadrupled rising from 7 to 26 per cent, compared to a rise from 8 to 18 per cent for teenage boys. While the youth share of total employment dropped by more than a tenth, their share of part-time work in the labour force increased by more than a third. Since 1981, while

Table 1. **Total and Part-time Employment August 1970 and August 1983**
Numbers are in thousands

Employment	15-19 years	20-24 years	15-24 years	25 years and over	15 years and over
1970 Total	623.5	814.3	1 437.8	3 957.8	5 395.6
1970 Part-time	49.0	51.3	100.3	469.4	569.7
1983 Total	564.9	908.7	1 473.6	4 759.1	6 232.7
1983 Part-time	158.2	99.8	258.0	828.4	1 086.4

Table 2. **Full-time Employment August 1970 and August 1983**
Numbers are in thousands

Full-time employment	15-19 years	20-24 years	15-24 years	25 years and over
1970	574.5	763.0	1 337.5	3 488.4
(%)	92	94	93	88
1983	406.7	809.0	1 215.7	3 930.5
(%)	72	89	82	83

part-time employment for older workers was shrinking as quickly as full-time employment, it declined less than half as quickly as full-time employment for young people. The proportion of teenage females in full-time work has declined nearly twice as quickly as the male proportion, and their proportion of part-time employment has increased more than twice as quickly. Young adult females did not experience a sharply faster deterioration in full-time employment than males, or a sharply faster increase in part-time employment – but that was because they had so much less full-time employment, and so much more part-time employment to begin with.

Much of the increase in part-time employment among young people can be attributed to increasing numbers of full-time students working. The proportion of teenagers in school full-time and working rose from 5 per cent in 1971 to 27 per cent in 1981. It rose from 15 to 37 per cent for young adults. In 1981, 75 per cent of the teenage part-timers, and 25 per cent of the young adult part-timers were full-time students[5].

But it is difficult to evaluate the full significance of the increasing tendency to mix full-time enrolment in education or training with part-time employment. While there has been a dramatic increase in part-time employment, the increase in enrolment in education and training has been only marginal. It is not clear if the increased incidence of combining part-time work and education has contributed to the slightly increased enrolment rates in full-time education. Nor is it clear who among full-time students is working part-time – whether it is less disadvantaged or more disadvantaged youths, or whether it is a phenomenon covering all groups of young people. Finally, it is not clear what the long-term effects of the growth in part-time employment are with respect to subsequent employment for those who are working part-time and attending school full-time.

The shift towards greater part-time employment and less full-time employment is worrisome for its impact on the quality of work and earnings. It reflects a shift of young people into lower-paying, lower-status, less stable jobs. Part of this has been due to declines in industries with full-time opportunities and concurrent growth in areas employing people more on a part-time basis. Part is also due to technological changes diminishing the need for low-skilled workers. The result is that the early work experience of some young people is increasingly in jobs which provide few skills that might be used in subsequent jobs. They are also in sectors that offer little opportunity for lateral or upward mobility; these jobs lack access to the kind of informal networks and internal labour markets that would lead to more stable, higher-paying, higher-status employment.

In the short run, the increasing incidence of part-time work appears to be contributing to underemployment and lower earnings for young people. In 1980, the latest year for which data are available, the average wage for teenage part-time workers was A$3.25 per hour, and their average work-time was slightly more than eleven hours per week. At that level, average weekly earnings for teenagers working part-time were about equal to the weekly junior unemployment benefit. This posed no conflict for the part-time workers who were also full-time students and therefore not eligible for unemployment benefits, anyway. But for those not in education or training full-time, there is no way to replace the earnings loss accompanying the decline in full-time jobs.

While part-time employment has little to offer, the diminishing full-time employment opportunities for young people show signs of offering even less. Not only are full-time opportunities for young people declining in absolute numbers and relative shares, but the structure of the full-time jobs that do remain is changing in a way that seems to be isolating some young people. Some of the industries where young people have been most heavily concentrated are declining, and their representation in certain occupational areas is moving in directions opposite from the rest of the workforce.

Between 1970 and 1983, while their share of employment declined by 20 per cent, the teenage share of full-time employment dropped by 34 per cent. This reflects shifts in both the sectors and the occupations in which youth full-time employment has been concentrated (see Tables 3 and 4). In 1981, the two industries employing the most young males on a full-time basis – wholesale/retail trade and manufacturing – were the ones that sustained the biggest employment drops in the preceding ten years. Though adult males were also heavily represented in both those areas, they were more evenly represented through other occupational areas. The pattern was not as clear for young women because of their larger share of part-time employment. They too were heavily represented in declining industries, but

Table 3. **Changes in Demographic Composition of Occupations 1971-1976**
Change in share (%)

	Male 15-19	Male 20-24	Male 25+	Female 15-19	Female 20-24	Female 25+
Professional, technical and related workers	−0.8	−2.3	0.0	−0.9	−0.6	4.6
Administrative, executive and managerial workers	0.0	−0.4	−2.2	0.0	0.0	2.6
Clerical workers	−1.8	−1.2	−0.4	−3.9	−1.2	8.5
Sales workers	0.2	−1.3	−1.4	0.7	−0.3	2.1
Miners, quarrymen and related workers	−1.2	−1.1	1.6	0.1	0.2	0.4
Workers in transport and communication	−1.0	−1.0	2.1	−0.9	−0.8	1.6
Tradesmen, production-process workers and labourers n.e.c.	0.6	−0.1	0.1	−0.4	−0.4	0.2
Service, sport and recreation workers	0.5	0.6	−0.6	−0.9	−0.2	0.6
Inadequately described or not stated	−0.3	−2.0	−15.2	0.5	1.3	15.7
Total workforce	−0.4	−0.9	−2.0	−0.8	−0.1	4.2

they were also more heavily represented in finance, real estate and business services, and community services, the two fastest growing sectors of the Australian economy. Evidence elsewhere indicates, however, that those sectors require lower skills and pay less[6,7]. They also are oriented towards employing many part-time workers. Shifts in the public sector workforce have hit young workers the hardest. While growing at a rate nearly four times that of the private sector, public sector employment of teenagers declined by a third.

Table 4. **Change in Employment Levels 1971-1976**

	Employment levels 1971	Employment levels 1976	Change in absolute number	Change in %	Ranking by size of growth
Professional, technical and related workers	(536 508)	(683 611)	1 476 103	+27	1
Administrative, executive and managerial workers	(348 872)	(381 325)	32 453	+9	6
Clerical workers	(830 408)	(954 880)	124 472	+15	2
Sales workers	(421 886)	(448 812)	26 926	+6	7
Miners, quarrymen and related workers	(33 887)	(31 672)	2 215	+7	9
Workers in transport and communication	(290 790)	(298 311)	7 521	+3	8
Tradesmen, production process workers and labourers n.e.c.	(1 680 890)	(1 728 640)	47 750	+3	5
Service, sport and recreation workers	(387 562)	(452 751)	65 189	+17	4
Inadequately described or not stated	(240 570)	(316 088)	75 518	+31	3
Total workforce	(4 771 173)	(5 296 090)	524 917	+11	

Evidence on the composition of different occupational groups indicates that young people are not gaining ground in the areas with high occupational growth. Between 1971 and 1976, the fastest growing occupational areas were for professional, technical and related workers: the share for teenage and young adults dropped across the board. The same thing happened with their share of clerical occupations, the third fastest growing and second largest occupational area.

One area where teenage and young adult males did gain was among service, sport and recreation workers. But the real value of this gain, like the value of gains for young females in the community services area, is diminished by the concentration of low-paying and part-time jobs in that area. Young males made their biggest gains among tradesmen, production-process workers and labourers, the biggest single occupational area. But it was also the slowest growing occupational area during that time.

Strategies for Improving Employment Opportunities

Right now Australia does not have enough jobs for young people, and, increasingly, the jobs that are available are part-time and marginal, many of them in declining industries and shrinking occupational areas. As the Australian economy recovers from the current recession, it appears that, at the margin, employment growth will be in areas that will not favour young people.

The examiners believe this situation calls for setting three goals:

- Better economic conditions to improve employment across the board;
- Education and training opportunities designed to ensure that the qualifications and skills of young would-be workers are adapted to changes in the structure of the available jobs in the future; and
- Selective employment initiatives and interventions to increase the youth share of overall employment growth.

The examiners recognise the importance of a healthy economy in reducing youth unemployment. But, healthy macro-economic conditions, while necessary for improving employment prospects for young people, alone, are insufficient. Selective interventions are needed to help direct growth in a way to benefit young people. Education and training policies represent one strategy for assuring that, as the nature of the economy changes, the qualifications of young people entering the workforce will also change. Education and training are discussed in detail in Chapter 3. Selective employment interventions are discussed below.

As a complement to aggregate job growth and education and training policies, the examiners recommend selective employment interventions whose goals should be to:

- Create jobs quickly for young people.

If young people keep their present share of employment, the Australian economy will need to generate four jobs in the aggregate to provide one job for a young person. In order to raise their share of new jobs, selective interventions are needed to target jobs for youth.

- Create jobs that young people can perform now.

At the margin, full-time job increases are moving more and more away from young people. There is a need for jobs in the short run that young people can enter now, and unlike the part-time jobs that are beginning to dominate the youth market, are more likely to provide skills and access to better jobs.

- To assure employment for certain groups of young people with especially severe disadvantages in the labour market.

Labour markets, when left alone, do not necessarily function in a socially equitable manner. Some groups may need the benefit of governmental intervention not only to help them gain the competences they need to find employment, but to overcome the prejudicial effects of discrimination on the basis of sex, race or age.

The examiners recommend three kinds of strategies for achieving these goals:

i) Giving high priority to young people in the allocation of existing jobs;
ii) Taking advantage of structural changes to increase overall employment;
iii) Creating new jobs for young people.

Reallocation of Existing Jobs

Australian authorities have two important leverage points with regard to hiring activities in the labour market: hiring for public service and hiring through the Commonwealth Employment Service (CES).

In view of the size of public service employment and the marked decline in the share of that employment for teenagers, Australian authorities should evaluate the need for positive discrimination in favour of teenagers.

In this regard, it would be useful to find out why the youth share of public service employment has declined so much. By one estimate, public sector employment growth would have been 70 000 higher for 15-20 year-olds in 1981 if they had kept their employment share during the preceding ten-year period of growth[8]. The authorities need to know if there were changes regarding demand for young workers or supply behaviour, or something else that interfered. They then need to make adjustments accordingly.

Australian authorities should set priorities for the Commonwealth Employment Service with respect to placing young people in jobs and placing females in traditionally male jobs, and enforce such priorities with performance targets.

Presently the CES is the source of referrals for filling approximately 30 per cent of all job vacancies in the Australian economy. But, aside from facilitating smooth functioning of the labour market, the CES should compensate for distortions in it. CES should use this market leverage for improving the chances of young people looking for jobs. It is particularly important that CES provide the assistance that girls and young women need to overcome employers' discriminatory hiring practices. The examiners recognise the fact that since employer use of CES for job referrals is voluntary, the CES must respond to employer needs and cannot sacrifice standards in its referral and recruitment processes. As the main outside influence on private hiring practices, however, the CES can exercise leadership in assuring that employers do not discriminate illegally, and in persuading them to change hiring practices. One strategy for improving the responsiveness of the CES to the needs of girls and young women would be to increase their training for senior level and management positions in CES. The Australian authorities might also borrow from the experience of Scandinavian authorities and establish "equity consultants" in the CES to review job vacancy announcements, counselling, and referral practices and assure that they do not discriminate on the basis of sex. Whatever is done to increase placements of females in traditionally male jobs, a record should be kept of CES performance and employers' hiring patterns.

In applying positive discrimination, it is not suggested that young workers be favoured at the expense of other groups. Rather, positive discrimination is intended to assure that young people get a proportionate share of employment opportunities by counteracting any existing administrative practices by CES and hiring practices by employers that discriminate against young people for reasons having nothing to do with *bona fide* job requirements.

Australian authorities should undertake further research, usable at the labour market level, to determine which sectors of the economy and which occupational areas show the most promise for growth. The CES should concentrate on placing young people in those areas with growth opportunities and refer them to declining areas only as a last resort.

Young people are the ones who are probably least likely to be able to exercise much mobility in moving to another job. They are the least likely to have the requisite occupational skills, work experience, knowledge of informal networks, and access to internal labour markets and are the ones who need help the most in avoiding jobs that lead nowhere.

The CES should refer young people to part-time employment only when i) *such employment is necessary to allow them to continue in education or training activities, and* ii) *such employment is adequately protected.*

The dramatic upsurge in part-time employment among young people is worrisome because it is apparently at the expense of some full-time employment and because it is increasingly marginal work. The CES should place in part-time jobs only those young people who are in education and training. Young people without such a background are too much in danger of becoming trapped in marginal jobs. Further, CES should make referrals only to those part-time jobs that have protection comparable to that which full-time workers receive with regard to work safety, injury compensation, health insurance, and so forth.

Obviously the CES should not be the only agent for steering young people around marginal jobs. Education and training institutions can provide the occupational skill and job search competences to increase the mobility of young people. However, it is important that CES practices do not undermine or work at cross purposes with the policies and programmes of other public agencies.

Structural Changes to Increase Employment

Young people could also benefit from structural changes that increase the overall level of employment. As indicated earlier, increasing overall employment depends first and foremost on macro-economic policies that spur growth. But there is also room for structural changes that can work to the benefit of young people by increasing the number of jobs available at a given level of economic activity and improving the operation of labour markets. These are discussed below. It is also possible to increase the demand for labour at a given level of economic activity through other structural policies that lower capital-to-labour ratios. Such policies could include the relative tax treatment of physical capital investment and human capital investment, and the relative incentives for research, development, and applications of new technology to save capital, material, energy or labour. They are not discussed here since they are beyond the terms of reference. Other structural policies for increasing the demand through more or different education and training are discussed in Chapter 3.

Three structural changes related to increasing overall employment prospects are working-time adjustments, wage adjustments, and increased availability and use of labour market information. The first two are discussed below because of their presumed importance as policy instruments affecting employment prospects. The third is of no direct importance for employment, but is discussed because it is critical in guiding the allocation of resources for training activities; it is important, therefore, for its potential indirect consequences.

In the OECD area, working time has been steadily reduced through shorter work weeks – the forty-hour week is standard almost everywhere – more vacation time and early retirement. Until the recession induced by the most recent oil shock, working time has been reduced as part of a general improvement in social welfare. Only recently has there been interest in reducing working time as a way of increasing employment. However, that interest has not been universal, and there is no consensus over which, if any, reduced working-time strategy will necessarily lead to more employment.

One approach is to reduce career working time by encouraging early retirement. The German government favours, and Denmark and France have adopted, schemes to encourage early retirement in the hopes that eventually this will open up entry-level jobs to young people. Since 1975, in Denmark, workers over 60 who are members of an unemployment insurance fund can choose to leave the workforce before the retirement age when they receive their pensions. Approximately 50 per cent of the jobs left vacant by early retirement are filled. It is not clear how many entry-level jobs for young people are eventually freed by this strategy. But the net cost of the strategy for young people appears to be manageable because the benefits paid to the "early retirees" are less than what they would receive on unemployment (which they would receive if they were sacked) or under their pensions. In 1982, the French authorities launched a more structured scheme of "solidarity contracts" under which the government offsets the costs to employers of early retirements if those are tied to hiring young workers. The scheme has been scrapped since then for being too expensive, though the French authorities are encouraging "pre-retirement". The usefulness and cost-effectiveness of this strategy in Australia is likely to depend in large part on demographic patterns (how many workers are reasonably close to retirement now?), and the value of benefit levels for old-age pensions versus the value of savings on unemployment and other income support benefits.

Another strategy for reducing working time is to shorten the work day so as to reduce total weekly work-time. France, Spain and the United Kingdom have adopted such measures. But the measures vary according to how work-time reductions are "paid for". In the United Kingdom, where working time is being reduced under collective bargaining agreements as a general strategy for improving the welfare of workers through shorter work weeks, the reductions are intended to be tied directly, wherever possible, to productivity increases. The schemes in France and Spain are tied less directly to productivity and geared more to spreading employment regardless of productivity gains. In other countries, such as Denmark and Germany, suggested schemes for shortening the work week are linked loosely to productivity growth, maintaining constant money income, but using cost of living "increases" to pay for fewer working hours. But here too there is a great deal of uncertainty about the extent to which shorter working hours for employed workers will lead to more employment, and the time required for such adjustments.

Despite the ambiguous results with work-time reduction measures, they continue to attract attention because of the pay-offs that some analysts expect. In Denmark, Social Democrats and trade union supporters of a shorter work week project a 30-60 per cent reduction in unemployment over five years if the working week is reduced over that time by five hours, without compensation for lost wages or reductions in capacity utilisation, and with appropriate training to prevent skill shortages. Belgian authorities estimated a 15 per cent reduction in unemployment if its package of working time adjustments had been adopted in 1983.

Nevertheless, working time adjustment options are controversial, not only because of uncertainty about their impact on employment levels and cost, but because of the differing points of views and objectives of the two parties concerned – workers and employers. In the OECD area, trade unions interested in consistently increasing employment and improving the welfare of workers favour shorter working hours though there are different points of view as to how to pay for those hours. Employers, arguing that shorter hours may increase costs, oppose a shorter work week for workers across the board, though there is strong employer support for "flexible" working hours.

In the view of the examiners, there is too much uncertainty to justify accepting or rejecting adjustments in work-time as a strategy for increasing youth employment. Moreover, they recognise the difficulty in making adjustments in working time in the context of the existing wage-fixing arrangements. But for two reasons, the examiners think working-time adjustments deserve further consideration:

i) In the medium term, working-time adjustments may improve employment prospects for young people when labour demand is slack. Any possibility of increasing employment needs to be considered carefully, because Australia is in no position to reject promising possibilities, in the hope of finding "sure-fire" remedies. A degree of uncertainty in labour market management policies is inevitable;

ii) In the longer term, shorter hours may be the only way to assure a job for everyone who wants to work, even in the healthiest economy. If high technology does indeed reduce the requirement for labour as much as many expect, a shorter work week may be the only way to avoid a dual society made up of those who work and those who do not. Without shorter hours over the longer term, there is a risk that the unemployed young people of the 1980s will become the first permanent members of an enforced leisure class.

Australian authorities should continue to monitor the experience of other countries regarding working-time reductions and consider further reducing working time, if other countries' experience warrants it, as a way of increasing employment opportunities for young people.

While recognising that the Commonwealth and state authorities have no direct control over the wages and hours negotiated in collective bargaining agreements, the examiners do believe that they can exercise a leadership role and set precedents in public service agreements.

The issue of working-time adjustments is substantively complicated and politically charged. Uncertainties about costs and consequences for youth employment and the presence of multiple objectives require policy-makers to be cautious in choosing their options. The question of increasing youth employment by reducing wages paid to young people has much clearer answers for policy-makers in the opinion of the examiners.

Australian authorities should not reduce youth award wages as a way of increasing youth employment.

Australia already has in place a wage structure that sets lower wages for youth presumably to reflect their lower productivity. The arguments for further adjusting youth wages downwards in order to increase youth employment are not persuasive. First, such a move risks trading youth unemployment for adult unemployment. Evidence on the effect of changes in youth-adult relative wages indicates that increased youth employment might come at the expense of displacing low-skilled adult workers[9]. Moreover, though there is evidence inside and outside Australia that compression of youth-adult wage differentials has a depressing effect on youth employment, the size of the effect is ambiguous[10]. To the extent compressed youth-adult wage differentials actually do reduce youth employment[11], the examiners believe the implied preference of employers for adults is for more skilled workers. The more appropriate response, then, is to raise skill levels with more education and training.

The need for more labour market information is alluded to at different points in this report; the need is probably most appropriately addressed as a labour market management issue though it is most badly needed in planning education and training activities.

Commonwealth authorities should expand the availability of labour market information and forecasts of occupational and skill requirements. This information should be developed for use at the state and labour market level.

There are two agents making education and training decisions that might have an impact on employment: the institutions providing education and training, and the consumers of those services, usually young people. Both lack occupational outlook, vacancy, and other labour market information usable at the state and labour market level. (See in particular the discussions in Chapter 3 on TAFE and secondary education guidance and counselling.) The examiners recognise that certain aggregate labour market and career planning information is available, and in at least one state, Western Australia, the Department of Employment and Industrial Relations is trying to adapt it to state-level conditions, for use by career educators and counsellors. But there are gaps in coverage, particularly at the local level. Moreover, there appear to be shortcomings in the usability of the available information, by young people especially. Limits on the availability and usability of labour market information make it difficult to make sound decisions about what is the most appropriate education and training for institutions to offer and what are the most appropriate occupations for young people to enter. The examiners believe that the Commonwealth should assume additional responsibility for seeing that such data are directly available to, and usable by young people. That phase of using labour market and career planning information is too technical and the information too perishable to place full responsibility within schools and training institutions.

While suggesting that the Australian authorities support more occupational forecasts, the examiners are well aware of the limits of developing and using forecasts. As a rule, forecasts are of limited usefulness in anticipating employment levels in different occupations, and consequent skill imbalances. They have wide margins for error because of their reliance on overall growth forecasts (which themselves have considerable margins of error), and their sensitivity to differences in growth between sectors and fluctuations in the distribution of occupations across sectors. To the extent forecasts of skill imbalances are correct, the usefulness of the information is limited by elements of flexibility in firms and in the application of skills by workers. Firms can adjust to skill imbalances by reorganising production, and the effective impacts of presumed imbalances can be mitigated by the extent to which skills are adaptable across occupations. However, forecasting can be useful if forecasts are published for different assumptions about economic growth, and if they reflect the consequences of different policies and developments regarding the growth and decline of particular sectors and the level of technology in use[12].

While recognising the limitations of techniques for forecasting manpower and skill requirements, the examiners recommend that Australian authorities push ahead in order better to articulate the relationship between economic growth and changing technology, on the one hand, and manpower and skill requirements, on the other. Making such information available and usable at the level at which planning for education and vocational training takes place, together with more input from employers and unions (see Chapter 3), should help provide a broader basis for those planning decisions, and ultimately make those activities more relevant to real labour market requirements. Similarly, occupational outlooks for local labour markets and information on the preparation required for various occupations should be made available to young people to help them make better informed career planning decisions. Finally, to the extent there are uncertainties about the accuracy of forecasts of occupational and skill demand, those uncertainties can emphasize the importance of extended education and broad-based training as a way to cope with change.

Creating New Employment

Whatever is done with respect to redirecting public and private sector hiring practices and increasing overall employment through structural changes, there will not be enough jobs for all the young people who want them, at least in the near term. Even if enrolment in education and training is increased and labour force participation falls, there will be young people who will want work, and of course, as others complete education and training, they will be looking for jobs as well. In 1982/83 about 80 000 young people were enrolled in the two principal work experience and training programmes – less than a third of the number of young people who were unemployed at the time[13]. In order to increase employment prospects for young people, the Australian authorities will have to do more job creation than they are doing already. But in supporting job-creation interventions, care needs to be taken with regard to who is employed and what kind of jobs are created.

Australian authorities should continue to target employment-generating programmes for the most disadvantaged young people, including youths unemployed for long periods of time, those early school-leavers who do not return to an education or training setting of any kind, and those living in areas with only limited employment opportunities.

As a general principle, public job-generating resources should be dedicated to those who are least likely to find employment without specific intervention on their behalf. The examiners commend the Australian authorities for targeting the current major job-creation initiative, the Community Employment Programme, more highly on those most at risk in the labour market than the previous Wage Pause Programme was targeted. But there should also be specific objectives regarding the placement of young people in subsidised jobs.

Publicly-supported jobs created to provide employment opportunities should have some legitimate and documented training content to them and, as much as possible, provide access to informal networks and internal labour markets that may lead to more permanent employment.

Short-term employment that leads nowhere is of little use to young people except as justification for income transfer. If nothing else, young people should be able to leave a temporary job with a certifiable competence to help them with further job search.

It may be more important, though, for temporary jobs to expose young people to networks of fellow employees to help them find employment elsewhere and even internal labour markets that offer routes for lateral mobility to more permanent jobs. At the very least, transition services should be provided to young people leaving subsidised jobs to help them find unsubsidised employment.

Besides creating jobs directly with subsidised employment projects, the Australian authorities should support development of job-generating "local employment initiatives".

In between the direct job creation carried out under the Community Employment Programme and the larger macro-economic policies designed to spur business growth, there are opportunities for greater government support of more innovative employment alternatives. Several countries in the OECD area have begun investigating and, in some cases, supporting ventures that have job creation as a major objective. These alternatives have ranged from unemployed persons trying to set up their own businesses to workers buying out factories scheduled for closure, to community co-operatives and other kinds of local initiatives designed to provide a social good. Support has been in the form of seed capital for furnishing the resources and for such technical aids as management assistance.

The common thread through all these ventures is that, though they can become largely or entirely self-supporting, they require an initial investment that they are unable to get because of their non-traditional organisational arrangements or management, or the non-traditional product they produce. Some represent collective community concerns that do not pool capital in the traditional entrepreneurial sense, but pool ideas and operate on democratic principles. Others follow a more traditional organisational approach to producing a not-so-traditional good in the form of social services or other leisure goods increasingly in demand in post-industrial societies. In both cases, the relatively novel objectives of such ventures – not just to maximise profits, but employment levels as well – blend private sector and public sector objectives, and may argue in favour of public/private capital partnerships.

Government can be an important source of "seed" capital for these ventures. The reason government interest is justified is linked to government support for more traditional small entrepreneurs in countries like Denmark, France, the United Kingdom and the United States: small businesses have been the major sources of employment growth (as well as important sources of technological innovation). Government can also play an instrumental role in fostering the kind of tax and regulatory climate that contributes to small business start-up and in encouraging instruction in "entrepreneurial" and business management skills in the context of vocational training. In Finland, France and the United States, this kind of training is already being provided alongside training for specific occupational skills. In Portugal, Sweden, Switzerland and the United Kingdom, government initiatives are also geared to providing training for small business management, but separate from vocational training.

These kinds of initiatives vary in their ability to succeed financially and in their labour intensiveness, particularly with regard to how much they can employ young workers and workers with few skills or inadequate education. In this regard, their likely viability and potential for expanding on the small-business base that already exists in Australia, can probably be evaluated – in part – on the basis of experience of small business to date.

As an adjunct to small business – traditional and non-traditional – as a base of expanded employment for young people, Australian authorities might also consider introducing "production schools". In place in Denmark and tested on a limited scale in the United States, these are institutions set up to provide occupational skill training in a production setting. The proceeds from sales of whatever is produced are typically used to offset operating costs and pay income support (allowances) to trainees. In order to be accepted and not displace potential employment that might have been available otherwise, these institutions need to be organised and their output needs to be such that there is no competition with local employers. (They are limited in Denmark, for example, to producing goods only for export.) This obviously limits their potential scale. But they may be feasible as small-scale, multi-purpose (training and employment) initiatives, particularly in isolated or economically depressed areas.

There is too much uncertainty and too little experience with the various small business initiatives to support them as major job-creation initiatives. But the experience so far in other countries warrants government support for experimentation to explore the feasibility of larger-scale initiatives and to provide a basis for evaluating the financial viability and the employment-generating capability of such ventures[14].

Conclusions

Young people in Australia face an immediate unemployment problem and the prospects of a more chronic and ominous underemployment problem.

The unemployment problem will benefit from better macro-economic conditions that improve employment in Australia overall. But Australian authorities should recognise that, for two reasons, a healthy economy is not enough to solve the problems of young people in the labour market:

 i) The sheer number of unemployed youths is so large that under even the best growth conditions, it will take an intolerably long time to create the needed jobs; and
 ii) New technology and shifts in the world economy are contributing to structural changes in the Australian economy that are sharply reducing employment opportunities for those young people with only limited education and occupational skills.

For these reasons, the efforts to improve the labour market experience of young people must entail two sets of policies. One, discussed above, is a set of selective labour market policies to augment the natural growth of jobs for young people that will accompany economic growth. The other, discussed in Chapter 3, is a set of education and training policies to make sure that young people are indeed equipped to take jobs in emerging sectors and growing occupations when they are available.

NOTES AND REFERENCES

Unless otherwise indicated, all data are taken from Department of Education and Youth Affairs, *Youth Policies, Programmes and Issues: An Australian Background Paper* (Australian Government Publishing Service, Canberra: 1983).

1. *OECD Employment Outlook* (Paris, 1984), p. 33.
2. OECD, *Economic Surveys 1982/83: Australia* (Paris, January 1983).
3. Youth deficit 1983 =
   [(Employment rate for 15-19 year-olds 1970) x (Labour force for 15-19 year-olds 1983)] − (Employed 15-19 year-olds 1983) =
   (0.57) (1 261.5) − (564.9) = 154
   (labour force and employment figures are in thousands)

   This allows for a lower labour force participation rate in 1983 than in 1970. If the deficit is calculated based on keeping the labour force participation rate in 1983 or the employment to population ratio in 1983 the same as in 1970, the deficit would be increased by about a tenth. Conversely, if increased education retention rates reduced teenage labour force participation rates from the current 57 per cent to 50 per cent, and perfect substitution of unemployed youth for employed youth who withdrew from the labour market were possible the deficit could be cut by more than half to 65 000.
4. (Youth deficit 1983)/ (Youth share of labour force 1983)
5. Paterson, P. and K. Mackay, *Working Paper Number 11 – Changes in the Youth Labour Market: 1971 to 1981* (Bureau of Labour Market Research, Canberra: 1982), pp. 5-9.
6. OECD, *Women and Employment: Policies for Equal Opportunities* (Paris, 1980).
7. Eva Cox, *Meeting Young Women's Needs* (Office of the Status of Women, Canberra: November 1983), pp. 66-68.
8. Bureau of Labour Market Research, *Youth Wages, Employment and the Labour Force* (Australian Government Publishing Service, Canberra: 1983), pp. 23-24.
9. John Martin, "Effects of the Minimum Wage on the Youth Labour Market in North America and France", in *OECD Economic Outlook, Occasional Studies* (OECD, Paris: June 1983).
10. Bureau of Labour Market Research, *Youth Wages, Employment and the Labour Force* (Australian Government Publishing Service, Canberra: 1983), pp. 94-95.
11. As the analysis of experience in Australia suggests for the period between 1970 and 1982 – *Ibid.*, pp. 49-53.
12. See OECD, *The Future of Vocational Education and Training* (Paris, 1983).
    Bundesminister für Bildung und Wissenschaft, *Neue Ansätze der Bedarfs und Qualifikationsforschung* (Bonn, 1984).
    U.S. Bureau of Labor Statistics, *1984-85 Occupational Outlook Handbook* (U.S. Government Printing Office, Washington, D.C.: 1984).
13. Department of Employment and Industrial Relations, *Submission to the Committee of Inquiry into Labour Market Programs: Factual Papers* (June 1984), pp. 69-81.
14. For more discussion see OECD, *Creating Jobs at the Local Level* (Paris: 1985). See also Keunstler, Peter, *Local Employment Initiatives: A View of the European Scene*, prepared for the International Seminar on the Contemporary Role of ILEs.

Chapter 3

EDUCATION AND TRAINING

Education and training are vital to Australia. They are necessary for guaranteeing Australians opportunity for social and economic mobility and for facilitating the process of assimilation by migrants to Australia into its culture and economic life. They are necessary to prepare the skilled workforce that Australia needs for further economic growth and to compete in a world economy.

The examiners found that, though there have been improvements in educational attainment and a substantial expansion of training capacity, education and training arrangements still do not serve well as tools for social equality or for meeting the skill and education requirements of Australia. The education and training arrangements in Australia are premised on the labour force needs of an industrial economy: a small minority of professional workers and highly-skilled trade workers, and a large majority of unskilled and semi-skilled manpower and skilled workers who learn their skills on the job; critical skill gaps have been filled through immigration. Such notions are dangerously obsolete in the post-industrial OECD economies where high technology and the service sector are growing in importance. Moreover, though the education and training arrangements do represent important actual and potential capacity, they are not easily managed as part of a public policy. There are critical gaps in the information needed to know what the arrangements are accomplishing now, and an inadequate sense of purpose for guiding policy.

The education and training arrangements are dominated by *i)* a lower secondary system geared to providing most young people with the basic competences they need to function as citizens and in a job requiring no technical skills for entry-level workers; *ii)* an upper secondary system that is geared to grooming students for higher education; *iii)* a higher education system (universities and Colleges of Advanced Education) for preparing professionals; *iv)* a technical training and further education sector (TAFE) for providing basic academic and further education, technical and non-apprentice-based vocational skill training, classroom training for apprentices, and cultural enrichment programmes; and *v)* an apprenticeship system for preparing highly-skilled craft workers.

There have been changes and additions to existing arrangements in recent years, though they have left the purpose of the mainstream institutions largely untouched. Over the last decade, the Technical and Further Education institutions have been greatly expanded in terms of the variety of course offerings and enrolment levels, to provide opportunities for institution-based occupational skill training, and enriching cultural and leisure activities. Since the mid-1970s and the rise in youth unemployment, the Commonwealth and some states have also supported special programmes better to prepare early school-leavers for employment. Additionally, in the 1970s, some schools began developing alternative programmes for students staying on through years eleven and twelve, but not matriculating for entry into higher education. Though the alternative programmes have been cited as examples of the kinds of changes needed in secondary education, they have had an uneven impact on increasing participation rates for years eleven and twelve. And, though the more recent innovations represented by TAFE and transition programmes compensate for certain shortcomings in the earlier education and training arrangements, they have not replaced but only augmented them.

Despite progress in improving the education and training arrangements, the changes have not gelled all of the pieces into a "system" in which there is *i)* a coherent overall sense of purpose that reflects the role of education and training in improving socio-economic equality and meeting the education and skill needs of the labour force through the end of the century; *ii)* a rational division of responsibilities among the parts for serving the overall purpose; and *iii)* formal points of transition between one institution and another. Without such coherence, it is difficult for the existing arrangements to serve as tools for assuring equitable access to development opportunities and for assuring that skill requirements of the economy are being met. The reasons for these shortcomings are probably most obvious at the level of young persons trying to negotiate their way through the institutions.

The most structured choice a young person can make is to opt for higher education. Students choosing it continue through levels eleven and twelve of the secondary schools, following courses of studies that are based on centrally-devised curricula that universities and colleges of advanced education require for admission, and having their competences evaluated in terms that are well established and used by higher education institutions for evaluating applications. For those who are admitted to higher study and complete it, the rewards are lower unemployment rates and somewhat higher earnings, though that edge is declining.

Young people going on to apprenticeships also follow a traditional route, although it entails moving outside the secondary school system. Typically, young people move into an apprenticeship position after year ten. The procedures for starting as an apprentice vary from state to state but usually involve finding an employer willing to establish an apprenticeship position and then having it approved by state apprenticeship authorities. Those in vocational programmes may receive help from school officials in finding an apprentice position, or in making the connection with state apprenticeship authorities. Sometimes, the state authorities or the Commonwealth Employment Service help locate interested employers. However, young people trying to go into apprenticeship are encountering increasing difficulties. In 1983, there was a 30 per cent drop in new apprentice positions and a large and growing number of trainees were retrenched due to economic circumstances. The vulnerability of apprenticeship to economic conditions limits such opportunities and for those who find placement, the option is less attractive than it once was.

The least structured choice young people can make is to leave school without moving into an apprenticeship position or on to higher education. This is what the majority of young people do. If they make the connection with TAFE, they can enroll in courses on topics ranging from cultural and leisure-time enrichment to occupational skill training and education geared to vocational preparation. Or they can enter the labour market. Those failing to find jobs may be able to enroll in one of a number of Commonwealth and state programmes for providing transition assistance, basic academic skills, or subsidised employment. But, in fact, young people who leave school before completing year twelve are very much on their own. The secondary schools are not suited to provide them with the counselling, career information, and career development information they need to make informed choices about what occupations they would like to pursue and what preparation they need to succeed. Nor are they always adequately equipped to carry on very effective job search or prepared to differentiate jobs with training opportunities or upward mobility possibilities from those that lack them. Moreover, the transition from secondary school to the principal alternative institution – TAFE – is an uncertain one. Despite the suitability of many TAFE courses of study for early school-leavers, formal transition provisions between secondary and TAFE institutions are virtually non-existent; transition depends instead on informal arrangements between secondary school and TAFE officials, or on the initiative of young people themselves.

From the point of view of social policy, the current arrangements are not equitable because those young persons with the least education and least preparation are thrust into the most unstructured situation requiring the broadest range of decisions. Since the most important determinant of educational achievement is socio-economic background, this set of arrangements reinforces patterns of inequality by channelling early school-leavers into an unstructured set of opportunities having a high probability of failure.

From the point of view of economic policy these deficiencies that are encountered first-hand by young persons are also symptomatic of more systemic deficiencies that limit the capacity of the current arrangements to meet the education and skill requirements of the Australian economy. The five most important deficiencies that need to be addressed are these:

- i) Retention in secondary education is low, and it is biased against adequate preparation of girls; those who leave school early are not adequately prepared for work or training or to make informed occupational choices;
- ii) There is too little connection between vocational training policies and labour market conditions and requirements; there are too few vocational training opportunities and, except for apprenticeship, competences gained from such training are not adequately evaluated and certified;
- iii) The apprenticeship system is biased against women, too vulnerable to fluctuations in economic activity, and is not sufficiently flexible to respond to changing skill requirements;
- iv) Job-based training, the only kind that many young people receive, is largely undocumented;
- v) Higher education opportunities are spread inequitably.

The following discussion examines the deficiencies in each of these areas, and the reasons for them, and proposes remedies for correcting them.

Secondary School Retention

The examiners find the apparent retention rates at the secondary level to be too low. Since the mid-1970s, retention through year twelve has edged up slightly but was still only 36 per cent in 1982. The rate for government schools was lowest of all secondary schools, at 30 per cent.

The examiners have two reasons for thinking these figures are too low and need attention. First, the alternatives to secondary school enrolment are not sufficient. The principal alternative, TAFE, enrolls young people mostly on a part-time basis, and even the value of that part-time enrolment is not certain. Second, the low retention rates are a signal that something is fundamentally wrong in secondary education. They indicate that nearly two-thirds of all young people would rather take chances with some very uncertain alternatives than to stay in secondary school. The examiners conclude that the decision of most young people to leave school reflects as much their disaffection for it as the attractiveness of the options. Moreover, the examiners believe that this dissatisfaction stems not only from expectations about what happens in years eleven and twelve, but is based on actual experience in year ten and much earlier.

Why is Secondary School Retention so Low?

The most important causes of low retention rates in years eleven and twelve seem to be a commonly accepted practice of early school-leaving, a lack of relevance of what is taught in years eleven and twelve to anything other than preparation for higher education, and an inflexible approach to the organisation and management of schools.

Secondary school retention and indeed enrolment in all post-compulsory education in Australia have always been low compared to enrolment in most other OECD countries (see Table 5). Though cross-country comparisons should be made carefully, it would appear that in the past, the Australian economy, because of its past relative isolation from world markets, simply has not required the level of skills needed in more heavily industrialised economies and those countries lacking the agricultural and mineral resources of Australia. Apprenticeship was adequate for supplying skilled trade workers. Certain critical shortages were met through immigration of skilled workers. Indeed, until the mid-1970s, most of the young persons who left school after year ten or eleven, lacking any formal recognised occupational skills, had little trouble finding jobs.

Table 5. **Participation Rates in Education and Training for 16-19 Year-olds**
Selected Countries 1981

Country		16		17		18		19	
		Total	Full-time	Total	Full-time	Total	Full-time	Total	Full-time
Australia	M	78.7	58.6	65.7	36.7	52.6	18.9	45.7	15.9
	F	75.7	63.8	52.6	40.4	32.4	18.8	29.0	16.7
Denmark[a]		86.0	n.a.	68.0	n.a.	61.0	n.a.	50.0	n.a.
France	M	83.6	66.8	69.4	52.7	45.2	42.2	30.0	29.4
	F	85.0	80.1	72.3	67.2				
Germany	M	92.1	57.5	89.3	39.3	74.9	26.7	47.6	19.1[a]
	F					65.6	32.1	42.6	24.1
Sweden[b]		77.9	n.a.	69.1	n.a.	35.8	n.a.	15.3	n.a.
United Kingdom[c]	M	66.9	37.9	56.4	24.6	44.0	15.5	32.8	14.0
	F	11.4	66.5	46.5	48.8	29.0	30.4	14.0	25.0
United States	M	94.6	n.a.	86.6	n.a.	57.4	n.a.	42.7	n.a.
	F	93.8		87.1		53.9		40.8	

a) 1980 figures.
b) All figures are for 1978.
c) All figures are for 1979.
Source: OECD educational statistics.

However, years of high unemployment seem to be changing the attitudes towards enrolment in education and training. They are becoming more important both for their credential value and for their intrinsic worth in preparing young people for emerging jobs. Surplus labour has made it a "buyer's market" for employers, allowing them to be more selective about who they hire; education and skill qualifications are convenient tools for screening job applications. But there is also more intrinsic value to education and training. The growing presence of high technology in the workplace – and the expectation of more – has also imposed new skill requirements that cannot always be met with employer-provided training. Jobs are getting more complicated and are requiring that workers enter the workforce with better qualifications. Discussions with young people, employers, and government authorities indicate that the need for more education and training is now widely accepted. Moreover, some argue that high youth unemployment might encourage young persons to stay on longer at school or to enroll more in training, simply because jobs are not available, and therefore the costs of attendance (in foregone wages, for example) are lower. This has been the experience in other OECD countries: at the same time that youth employment has been declining, their enrolment in education and training has risen. But, contrary to expectations, there have been only slight increases in educational and training enrolments of young people in Australia (certainly less than the increases seen in other OECD countries), with girls showing the largest and steadiest of those increases. Some have also suggested that in the face of poor job prospects and the expectation of worsening prospects, and possibly mindful of the decreasing or uncertain financial returns to higher education, many young people, particularly those who would have gone on to higher education, are trying to find employment sooner than they would have otherwise in order to get established in a job.

The examiners see merits in these arguments but conclude also that the nature of secondary education itself is part of the reason for low retention rates. Specifically, secondary education is not relevant to those young people who are not interested in going on to higher education, and the organisation and management of secondary education is too rigid for many young people.

Despite efforts under the School-to-Work Transition Programme, the Participation and Equity Programme, and some independent attempts to create education alternatives in years eleven and twelve, secondary education has little to offer a young person who is not going on to higher education. The courses are geared to the entry requirements of universities and colleges of higher education, and have little to do with the working world or the skills required on a job. Student assessment is based heavily on the screening needs of those institutions. Students who stay through year twelve leave with no more education or training oriented to help them in the labour market than they would have after year ten, though the higher school certificate may give them a competitive edge over other job-seekers. Many young people also find schools unattractive because schedules are rigid. They have no control over what they do, and they generally find school to be an overly structured experience that is shaped taking little account of what young people want. Some further changes obviously are needed.

Secondary schools also appear to be slipping in the preparation they provide for girls in particular. Though girls are slightly more likely than boys to stay through year twelve, the advantage is diminishing. Secondary schools continue to steer girls into long-term career development paths that channel them into lower-paying, lower-status jobs. Evidence indicates that girls in years eleven and twelve are under-represented in the science, math, design and technology courses that are typically required to enroll in science and engineering courses in higher education. They are over-represented in the arts and humanities[1]. Moreover, though girls 17-19 years old are slightly more likely than boys to be enrolled in higher education, the gap appears to be narrowing, and not entirely because more boys are going on to higher education. Girls who stay through year twelve are less and less likely to continue on to university or colleges of advanced education. The proportion starting higher education after year twelve declined from 52 to 40 per cent between 1976 and 1982. While rates for the progression to higher education were declining overall during that period, they declined at a rate for girls that was more than three-fourths higher than the rate for boys. In light of the powerful influence of secondary education in shaping the career plans and dictating occupational choices of girls, more needs to be done to assure that their school experience is balanced compared with boys.

Improving Secondary Education

The examiners' greatest concern with secondary education in Australia is with its quality and relevance. They commend the Australian authorities for the initiatives they have taken to improve secondary education. The work of the Commonwealth Curriculum Development Centre to broaden and improve secondary school curriculum is being continued. The new Commonwealth Participation and Equity Programme improves on the School-to-Work Transition Programmes, by explicitly aiming to improve the content of secondary education offerings, so as to increase retention at the secondary level, and in particular raise achievement and retention for disadvantaged students, the ones who do worst presently.

But though the interest and resources for improving secondary education are there, the specific content of such reform is not entirely clear.

The examiners, recognising and endorsing the steps that have already been taken, recommend five specific courses of action for improving the quality and relevance of secondary education and increasing school retention in order to make it more attractive to young people, especially those not going on to higher education.

i) *Improve curriculum and course offerings*

Any improvements in curriculum and course offerings must rest squarely on the assumption that retention through year twelve is useful for many young people, not just those going on to higher education. Because upper secondary enrolments have usually consisted of young people going on to higher education, secondary education is heavily oriented towards helping to facilitate the transition by concentrating instruction on courses required for entrance to higher education institutions. Improvements must then be geared to doing what is necessary to make secondary education productive and enjoyable enough to a broader cross-section of young people in order to raise retention voluntarily.

Two general kinds of changes are needed. There should be a wider selection of courses (beyond those usually required for higher education) and more flexibility and adaptability in instructional techniques to accommodate different learning styles and educational objectives. The examiners urge that improvements be based, in part, on increasing emphasis on the practical applications of what is learned and drawing the upper secondary level closer to the workplace. This might be accomplished by allowing greater flexibility in creating new "learning environments". These changes could include students spending more time in a workplace, team teaching that involves pairing instructional staff with persons from industry and government, and use of computer-based instruction. Changes in content of secondary curricula are also needed. In modifying existing courses and adding new offerings, it would be helpful to orient curricula more towards the outside world and the world of work. In this respect, secondary schools should expand the use of link courses to provide students interested in vocational training in TAFE with the opportunity to integrate such training with secondary school curriculum.

In accomplishing changes, the Australian authorities should also consider tapping the expertise and experience of non-traditional and community-based providers for ideas on the subjects, curricula and educational approach that might be adopted in order to improve retention. There are useful examples of how the experience in years eleven and twelve can be adapted to the interests and needs of young people who are not necessarily going on to higher education. The mixed vocational and general education approach found in the technical high schools in Victoria and at least one vocational high school in South Australia appear to succeed in retaining students through year twelve, who are not going on to higher education. In South Australia, the state Departments of Education and Labour are joint sponsors of a community improvement youth programme now active in a limited number of high schools to provide life and work skills to students in years eleven and twelve who are not going on to higher education. Finally, although the Community Youth Support Scheme projects (CYSS) appear to have a mixed record of effectiveness (due in part to low funding levels), many have been remarkably effective in generating community support and creating the kind of community-based setting that might be adapted to educational purposes, using the community involvement model of CYSS, or CYSS projects themselves as alternative education deliverers.

ii) *Increase "life skills" preparation and vocational counselling, and increase the availability of occupational outlook information and guidance on career preparation: all of this should be provided with a greater emphasis on breaking down sex-role stereotyping*

Another ingredient for making secondary education relevant to the needs of young people, particularly those not going on to higher education, is counselling and experience that better equip young people to solve problems, make decisions for themselves, manage their finances, find employment and plan careers.

These kinds of "survival" skills and work orientation training typically provided by community-based organisations such as some Community Work Support Scheme projects and Education Programme for Unemployed Youth projects provide exactly the kind of preparation from which high-risk youth would benefit. Those are the kind of offerings needed at the upper secondary level to retain those young people beyond years ten and eleven.

The examiners also found a need for more labour market data and career information to make young people aware of the education and training needs for different occupations and to help them make informed decisions about the careers they would like to pursue. Of course, for this to happen, data usable at the labour market level need to be available. That is something which state and Commonwealth Department of Employment officials ought to provide. But there is also a need for information regarding the skill, education and training requirements for different occupations.

There is a more basic need (that does not require labour market data) to encourage girls to consider "non-traditional" occupations and to get the appropriate preparation in secondary school. It is especially important that girls going on to years eleven and twelve enroll in courses that will help them meet entrance requirements for higher education courses that lead to higher-paying, higher-status jobs.

iii) *Make assessment and credentialing of secondary education more adaptable*

Just as the courses and content of secondary education are geared to preparing students for eventual enrolment in higher education, the current assessment and credentialing practices are also dominated by the screening and assessment requirements of higher education institutions. Student performance is evaluated too much according to criteria that higher education institutions need for screening applicants. Not only must secondary schools encourage a broader definition of educational attainment, they should be able to assess a broader set of educational outcomes. If secondary schools are to retain students who are not bound for higher education, there needs to be more adaptability in assessing and credentialing secondary education in order first to evaluate competences in a way that is usable to employers and young people themselves. The addition of new courses that are not part of the preparation for higher education will also require different assessment and credentialing practices since they would not be part of the usual higher education preparatory courses.

    iv)   *Give students a greater voice in the organisation and management of secondary education*

For most young people, the end of their secondary schooling marks the end of their formal education; for many it marks the transition into adulthood. It would be helpful for secondary schools to prepare young people for making their own decisions and assuming responsibility for their lives by allowing them to participate more in deciding what courses and educational activities are offered, how they are taught, and how competences are evaluated.

    v)   *Extend improvements well below the upper secondary level*

Because the examiners believe that secondary education experience in year ten and earlier has an impact on the decision to leave school early, improvements cannot be confined to years eleven and twelve. The kinds of changes described above should be applied to lower secondary education. In particular, it is essential that the young people who do leave after year ten have had some opportunity for vocational exploration, and are familiar with the use of labour market information and career counselling resources in looking for employment and making future decisions about education and training.

In trying to bring about reforms in secondary education, the authorities will almost certainly have to take into account the impact of the private, non-governmental schools sector. Parochial and other non-governmental schools enroll a significant proportion of all students in Australia; in 1982 they enrolled 28 per cent of all secondary students[2], and slightly more than a third of all those in years eleven and twelve. The high proportion of year eleven and twelve students in non-governmental schools and the higher representation of students from these schools in higher education means that there are strong incentives for private schools to maintain current academically-oriented curricula. Under these circumstances authorities will need to take special care that reforms designed to broaden the options of students not going on to higher education, are not perceived as lowering standards overall. The reforms should clearly expand choices through year twelve for those not going on to higher education, by adding to what is already provided, not replacing it.

Expanding and Improving Post-Compulsory Vocational Training Opportunities

Australia does not appear to have adequate vocational training resources. The examiners found clear evidence of too few training places, reason to question the appropriateness of training that is offered, and little evidence about the cost-effectiveness of certain current training expenditures.

Australia certainly lacks the capacity to accommodate everyone who is interested in training, and it appears to lack the capacity to accommodate the skill demands of a healthy economy. Outside the apprenticeship system (which is discussed later), the Technical and Further Education (TAFE) system is the most important institutional resource for vocational training. It also provides further education and non-vocational courses. Despite its rapid growth (a 35 per cent increase in enrolments from 1975 to 1980, and a 29 per cent increase in spending over the same period), TAFE and other officials report that the number of persons seeking enrolment consistently outstrips current capacity by a wide margin. Queensland TAFE officials estimate that demand is nearly double what the system can actually accommodate. A large part of the over-demand for TAFE can no doubt be attributed to low secondary school retention rates. Many early school-leavers enroll in TAFE, and if secondary retention were improved, some of the demand for it might fall.

It is also probably fair to conclude that, regardless of current demand among would-be students for training, the Australian economy needs a larger number of technically-skilled persons. It is difficult to compare enrolments in training across countries because of differences in definitions of training and difficulties in distinguishing training from other forms of post-compulsory education. But based on a comparison of education and training participation rates in other countries (and the concern in those countries with increasing education and training), it would appear that Australia should be doing more than it does now. The current and likely future structure of the Australian economy is comparable to that of other countries; yet the level of training in Australia is considerably lower. Further, the information that is available on occupational outlooks and expected supply and demand, forecasts shortages in certain areas where TAFE training is now provided, or probably would be suitable (particularly in some trade and service occupations)[3].

The most sensible approach to expanding vocational training opportunities seems to be through TAFE. It is already a large system that is geographically dispersed enough to provide good access for most young people. Indeed, there is strong support at the state and Commonwealth level for expanding the TAFE system in part because of the apparent success of the system in attracting early school-leavers. But, no doubt, some of the support for expanding TAFE is also due to the fact that it is easier to change institutions by adding on than it is to first undo what is already in place, and then make changes – which is exactly the process of educational improvement that secondary schools must go through. In this regard, the examiners are concerned that any expansion of TAFE does not detract from the essential agenda for secondary school improvement.

More important, though, the examiners have certain misgivings about the current capacity of the TAFE system and the changes that are needed as part of such expansion. These concerns are listed below and discussed in the following section:

  i) Certain occupational skill training courses may not be entirely relevant to what is required in the workplace;
  ii) Female participation in TAFE is low and poorly balanced among the different streams of study;
  iii) There is insufficient documentation on exactly what TAFE is accomplishing now in terms of the number of persons served by the system, the intensity of services for those persons, the exact content of courses in which they receive training, and what happens to them after training;
  iv) There seems to be little consistency or standardisation in the content of courses in similar trade areas across different TAFE institutions or in the way that competences are evaluated.

The Relevance of TAFE Training

The examiners are concerned about whether the occupational skill training provided by TAFE indeed meets the skill requirements of the labour market. Their concern stems from the lack of arrangements for soliciting and considering the views of employers and unions in deciding what courses to offer, their content, techniques for assessing student competences, and standards for completion of training. Part of the success of apprenticeship is the role played by employers and unions regarding these issues. The examiners think there is a need for their greater involvement in TAFE courses than currently exists.

Under the current TAFE management and planning arrangements in at least some states there is too much of a risk, particularly at the individual college level, of training decisions being based on a variety of institutional considerations, rather than on how that training is likely to be used in the labour market. Despite the unique TAFE position of being in an "intermediary" role between tertiary education and the world of work, it appears that the main channels of communication of TAFE authorities are with other TAFE and tertiary education authorities. More employer and union involvement would help balance decision-making.

But under current arrangements for such involvement, they are limited mostly to a role that has little effect on the factors governing the relevance of training. Presently, formal involvement of employers and unions is confined to the process of reviewing TAFE building and operating plans. In this respect, systematic employer and union involvement seems to take place mostly at the state and Commonwealth levels and revolves around funding levels and funding-allocation decisions. It is a necessary function, but by itself it is far from sufficient for assuring that TAFE enrollees in occupational programmes are appropriately trained. The State and TAFE Councils (or equivalent governing bodies) and the TAFE Council on the Commonwealth Tertiary Education Commission also are influenced by state training authorities, as well as by the National Training Council and its Industry Committees on issues regarding the appropriateness of training. But, a strongly *centralised* role for employers and unions is not sufficient. Because of the diversity among TAFE institutions in course offerings, the degree of independence among those institutions in deciding how to manage training, and the relatively loose central management control, even strong employer and union involvement at the State and Commonwealth level has little impact on what happens in individual TAFE institutions.

The examiners recommend that Commonwealth and state TAFE authorities regularly survey employers and unions for their views on the appropriateness of TAFE training. As part of this assessment, TAFE authorities should also follow up samples of TAFE trainees to evaluate how they are training, whether they are in jobs related to their training, and how appropriate the training is in helping them perform their jobs.

The real test of the relevance of occupational skill training is what it contributes to a person's ability to work in an occupational area and adjust to changing conditions. Measuring that, though, is difficult under any circumstances and will be especially hard during an economic downturn when many persons trained in TAFE are likely to be unemployed. Employer and union views and the post-training experience of TAFE enrollees could provide some insights.

The examiners recommend more systematic involvement of employers and unions at the individual TAFE institution level, to elicit their views on the choice and content of occupational training courses, the techniques for assessing student competences, and standards for completion.

Local Labour Market Committees or some other bodies representing employers, unions, and TAFE institutions might be established better to assure that TAFE training policies take cognizance of the skill requirements of local economies.

No matter how relevant TAFE training may be, the examiners are convinced that relevancy can be improved with greater input from employers and unions.

Under-enrolment of Females

Because TAFE occupies such a prominent place in the vocational training arrangements, the examiners believe that it is essential that girls and young women have access to all its training resources. Unfortunately, as far as can be determined from the available data, female enrolments in TAFE are low and concentrated in the wrong places (see Table 6).

Table 6. **Participation Rates in TAFE**
Figures are in percentages

	Full-time 1975	Full-time 1982	Part-time 1975	Part-time 1982	Total 1975	Total 1982
15-16 year-olds						
Males	0.7	2.1	9.3	12.1	10.0	14.2
Females	2.4	3.1	4.8	8.1	7.2	11.2
17-19 year-olds						
Males	2.4	4.1	26.6	26.2	29.0	30.3
Females	2.2	3.8	7.9	10.2	10.1	14.0
20-24 year-olds						
Males	0.7	0.9	n.a.	11.6	n.a.	12.5
Females	0.4	0.7	n.a.	6.3	n.a.	7.0

For nearly all age groups, male participation rates in TAFE outpace female rates. Only 15-16 year-old girls participate more than boys and the advantage is slight. In most other cases, male participation rates are 25 to more than 100 per cent higher. On the positive side, as TAFE enrolments have grown, so have female enrolments, and at a pace faster than for males. Between 1975 and 1982, enrolments for 15-16 year-old girls grew at a rate of 56 per cent compared to 42 per cent for boys. It grew at a rate of nearly 40 per cent for 17-19 year-old girls, while growing less than 5 per cent for boys.

But the value of the rising female enrolments in TAFE is uncertain, at best. Females of all ages are under-represented in the most rigorous vocational streams of study, comprising only 7.1 per cent and 4.4 per cent respectively of the Basic Trade and Post-Trade Streams. These are the streams associated with apprenticeship, and the under-enrolment of females reflects their low participation in apprenticeship. But females are also under-represented in the Para-professional Stream, the streams that are aimed towards persons in middle-level and technical occupations. Females are slightly over-represented in the Preparatory and Other Skilled Streams, the streams emphasizing the most basic vocational and academic skills.

TAFE authorities should take steps to raise overall female enrolments in TAFE, and to raise their enrolment levels in the Para-professional, Basic Trade and Post-Trade Area.

Achieving such goals requires more than simply setting targets. TAFE authorities need to consider extraordinary counselling and guidance arrangements for encouraging females to enter training for traditionally male-dominated occupational areas. Some might be based on follow-up studies on the earnings of TAFE graduates from different streams. TAFE institutions certainly may have difficulty in raising female enrolments in trade streams as long as females are under-represented in apprenticeship. But they should take steps to assure that females enrolled in "non-traditional" trade training have access to the extra counselling and support they may need, particularly if they are only small minorities in the training classes.

Furthermore, counselling activities in both state and federal employment and education agencies, and the Commonwealth Employment Service also need to be orchestrated to do a better job of referring females to TAFE for training in these areas.

In any event, TAFE authorities should collect and publish more complete data on female enrolments by age and stream, showing enrolment trends over time, so that they can better gauge the effectiveness of measures for improving opportunities in TAFE.

The Need for More Management Information on TAFE

A third concern the examiners have regarding the TAFE is the lack of comprehensive and definitive documentation on its activities and what it is accomplishing, and what its real potential is. The examiners, fully cognizant of the difficulties of collecting detailed statistics from a system as large and decentralised as TAFE, nonetheless did not find convincing evidence that *i)* TAFE was already effective in providing technical training and education (though it is successful in attracting students, on a part-time basis at least), or *ii)* expansion of TAFE capacity would yield more of a pay-off than if, for example, the resources needed for such an expansion were devoted to secondary education or the support of enterprise-based training. The difficulty in documenting the case for TAFE stems from the lack (or unavailability) of detailed data on specific activities and results. The examiners had difficulty finding out exactly what young people are doing in TAFE or how expensive it is relative to other options. National TAFE statistics are available on enrolment by stream, but there is variability among TAFEs in what is involved in different streams. There is variability within TAFE institutions regarding what individual students in the same stream might be taking and the significance of completing particular studies. This means that the available data do not begin to provide a complete picture of what goes on in TAFE. Most importantly, there is also a lack of information on what happens with regard to further education or training, employment, or earnings, when students leave TAFE. This is a particularly important question given the high incidence of part-time enrolment and the general variability in the amount of time students actually spend in TAFE: 84 per cent of students under 19 years old and 94 per cent of those 20-24 years old, were enrolled for fewer than 540 hours of class attendance a year (see Table 7). Overall, nearly half of all students in TAFE are enrolled for fewer than 120 hours a year (see Table 8).

Without such information on what is going on in TAFE now, it is difficult – for the examiners and Australian authorities – to appreciate the actual role that TAFE plays in

Table 7. **Young Students within Each Stream by Contact Hours: 1982**

Streams	19 years and under				20-24 years			
	Less than 540 hours		540 hours or more		Less than 540 hours		540 hours or more	
Professional	671	(78%)	188	(22%)	643	(82%)	140	(18%)
Para-professional	31 788	(73%)	11 909	(27%)	46 986	(91%)	4 627	(9%)
Basic Trade	99 637	(93%)	7 831	(7%)	18 543	(97%)	649	(3%)
Post-Trade	6 031	(94%)	375	(6%)	10 136	(99%)	118	(1%)
Other Skilled	40 571	(79%)	10 965	(21%)	36 131	(98%)	919	(2%)
Preparatory	52 671	(82%)	11 315	(18%)	21 737	(89%)	2 554	(11%)
Total	231 369	(84%)	42 583	(16%)	134 176	(4%)	9 007	(6%)

Source: Commonwealth Tertiary Education Commission, *Selected TAFE Statistics: 1982* (February 1984).

Table 8. **Students with Fewer than 120 Contact Hours per Year: 1982**

Stream	Number	Percentage of all students in stream
Professional	1 601	54%
Para-professional	71 967	36%
Basic Trade	5 526	5%
Post-Trade	15 725	51%
Other Skilled	148 608	69%
Preparatory	110 571	63%
Total	353 998	47%

Source: Commonwealth Tertiary Education Commission, *Selected TAFE Statistics: 1982* (February 1984).

meeting the skill requirements of the Australian economy and providing a real opportunity for its trainees. It is also difficult to be confident about the significance and impact of possible policy changes.

There is a need for more definitive data on what happens to trainees when they leave, and a need for relating such outcome data to the kind of training received and the amount of time spent in training.

The examiners fully appreciate the danger of imposing administrative reporting requirements; they require time and resources and could impinge on the flexibility that seems to be part of the success of the TAFE system. The examiners also commend the state and Commonwealth authorities for the progress that has already been made in developing a national statistics base for a very decentralised system. But more is needed. Deficiencies noted in an earlier review of TAFE[4] persist. Perhaps it is not essential to have nationally comparable statistics. But it seems essential for such statistics to be available on a state-wide level so that resource-allocation decisions can be made with better understanding of their consequences.

Standards

Finally, the examiners find that competences are not being evaluated in a way that has meaning to employers and unions, and to trainees themselves. The approach to documenting competences in TAFE is to indicate whether a trainee has completed an area of study. This approach poses problems outside apprenticeship because there is no commonly accepted understanding of what "completion" really means because the length and content of courses can vary from institution to institution. The apprenticeship system gets around this by having a well-specified set of activities and well-specified procedures for evaluating trainee competences. Apprenticeship also benefits from a long history and a sound reputation.

Australian authorities should develop standards by which the competences of TAFE enrollees can be evaluated.

The examiners are aware of the difficulty of developing and applying standards for measuring training competences. But they are needed badly. Development of such standards might benefit from work in other OECD countries. Authorities in the United Kingdom (and elsewhere) have gone to some lengths to try to determine exactly what competences young people need for employment and then how best to measure them. Their interest has been motivated by the need to come up with measures of job-readiness for participants in the Youth

Training Scheme[5]. The Job Corps Program in the United States has been another watershed for work on the development of competence-based instruction for a high-risk youth. In the late 1970s, the United States Department of Labor launched an especially ambitious effort for developing and evaluating a range of competence-based instructional programmes (many using computer-assisted instruction for students and computer-managed testing and lesson assignment by teachers) for Job Corps enrollees, many of whom had minimal verbal and math competences. Development of competence-based instruction (and standards for evaluating competences) has gone furthest with regard to academic competences. Though there are standards for evaluating the job-readiness competences typically taught in Job Corps (and other youth employment preparation programmes), the real value of those competences in securing and holding jobs is still open to some dispute. Nevertheless, the basic approach developed in Job Corps has gained considerable credibility and popularity among educators and vocational trainers working with high-risk youth. This experience too might be applicable to the development of standards for evaluating competences[6].

Standards should probably be developed on a centralised basis. TAFE institutions might be left free to develop their own techniques for assessing competences with regard to such standards, based on trainee needs, teaching approaches, and course content.

Overall, the examiners had a positive impression of TAFE. It enrolls large numbers of students over broad geographical areas. It is accessible and appears to succeed in enrolling considerable numbers of young people who have lost interest in secondary education. These facts alone do not justify expanding TAFE, though.

An expansion of TAFE requires that a stronger case be made about its effectiveness. Yet, in looking for harder and more detailed evidence of the TAFE record, the examiners found many unanswered questions revolving around the three discussed here: Is TAFE occupational training relevant? Exactly who is in training and for precisely what are they being trained? What can trainees do when they finish training? Where are they, say, six months after? Without answers to these questions it is likely to be difficult to manage an expansion of TAFE and to be confident about the likely impact of such an expansion on improving opportunities for young people and meeting the skill requirements of the Australian economy.

Work-Based Training

The workplace is still the most important resource for occupational skill training in Australia. It always has been, and any TAFE expansion notwithstanding, it should continue to be. Work-based training covers a full range of activities that vary with respect to factors such as their degree of structure, the transferability of skills and means of finance. At one end of the continuum there is highly structural, formal apprenticeship training mixing theoretical, classroom-based instruction and work experience. At the other end, there is uncredentialed, informal training that workers receive at the workplace.

In reviewing the arrangements for work-based training opportunities for young people in Australia, the examiners concentrated on apprenticeship. It is a well-established and important training institution, being the port of entry to the labour force for approximately a quarter of all young men and a seventh of all young people. But it is also deficient in many respects. The discussion that follows critiques the present apprenticeship arrangements and suggests remedies for improving work-based training that include improvements in apprenticeship as well as some alternatives that borrow from the less structured modes of work-based training.

Apprenticeship, like any formal training, already serves two roles. One is to provide training. The other is to provide control access to employment by providing the "credential" required for certain work. The examiners find the existing apprenticeship system to be deficient in both respects:

   i) In controlling access to certain parts of the labour market, apprenticeship contributes to socio-economic inequality by effectively excluding women from the system. It under-enrolls females in traditionally male jobs and has failed to develop apprenticeships for traditionally female jobs.
   ii) Apprenticeship is of limited effectiveness as a training resource because the quality of training is not always adequate, the system is not very adaptable in responding to changing skill requirements, and because apprenticeship intakes fluctuate too much with variations in short-term economic conditions.

The examiners support apprenticeship in principle, viewing it as a valuable potential resource for training skilled workers and as an avenue of access to sound employment opportunities. But the deficiencies in the present arrangements are serious and undermine the effectiveness and fairness of the system. There is little point in keeping apprenticeship if these deficiencies are not corrected. But what would be worse if the present system is left unimproved is that alternatives to apprenticeship might evolve, alternatives that might compete for scarce resources and lead to wasteful duplication. Most seriously, though, a competing alternative could lead to a "dual system" of trade training, providing exclusionary and non-exclusionary training and employment opportunities, and a mechanism for discriminating eventually against persons in the labour market. The discussion below presents the most important deficiencies that the examiners found in apprenticeship arrangements.

Under-enrolment of Females in Apprenticeship

Despite its status as a major, publicly-financed training resource, apprenticeship in Australia is segregated, reserved almost exclusively for boys and young men. Fewer than one in ten new apprentices in Australia are female. Girls who are in apprenticeship typically are clustered in two trade areas: hairdressing (over 90 per cent female) and food services. They are almost totally absent from the other trade areas. For example, in New South Wales females represented less than 1 per cent of the apprentices in trades outside hairdressing in 1979-80. The examiners are concerned about this under-representation of females in apprenticeship because it aggravates socio-economic inequality. In the apprenticeable trade areas, those who have gone through apprenticeship training typically get the better paying, more stable, and higher-status jobs. The fact that women are under-represented in those occupations translates directly into under-representation of females in higher-paying occupations. This occupational segregation by sex is an important factor in explaining the overall earnings differentials in Australia, which show overall that average weekly earnings for women are 78 per cent of the average for men, and 72 per cent within the trades area[7]. The continued exclusion of females from apprenticeship perpetuates these patterns of inequality.

Under-representation of females in apprenticeship reflects two conditions that need to be addressed by the Australian authorities. First, most apprenticeable trades are male-dominated. This is because apprenticeship authorities, associated training institutions, and employers apparently discourage females from entering certain trade areas, and because girls and young women are not interested in entering male-dominated trade areas (the second case is, probably in part, a product of the first). Second, only one occupation that is predominantly female is covered by apprenticeship. The first problem requires measures to increase female enrolments in the existing, traditionally male, apprenticeships. The second problem suggests creating apprenticeship positions in new trade areas. Remedies are discussed below.

So as to increase female enrolments in traditionally male-dominated trade areas, Australian authorities should adapt a three-pronged strategy of positive discrimination aimed at apprenticeship authorities, training authorities and employers; special support measures for females in apprenticeship; and special counselling measures to encourage girls and young women to enter trade training that has been dominated by males.

Positive compensatory discrimination measures are needed to force changes in past, unfairly discriminatory pratices. The recently enacted federal legislation against sex discrimination certainly will help, as will the financial incentives that the Commonwealth has introduced to encourage employers to take on female apprentices. But there is a range of institutional rigidities that also need to be addressed if lasting changes are to be achieved. At least part of the reason why there is low enrolment of females in apprenticeship is because of well-entrenched historical patterns, and because there has been little reason – in the form of incentives or sanctions – to change. Positive discrimination measures are essential to force changes, regardless of what else is done.

As a first step, Commonwealth and state authorities should require state apprenticeship authorities to report regularly on enrolments in different trade areas broken down by sex. A second step would be to establish "performance goals", target enrolment levels for females in different trade areas.

Special support measures are needed so that once females are enrolled as apprentices, they have a reasonable chance of succeeding.

Australian authorities should consider separate pre-apprenticeship and apprenticeship training courses for girls in those occupational areas where they fail to achieve a balanced enrolment of males and females.

If girls are to be retained in non-traditional apprenticeship areas, extraordinary measures are likely to be necessary *i)* to compensate for the different background that females are likely to have, and *ii)* to provide some degree of "shelter" from the pressures from male students, instructors, and employers that are virtually unavoidable for females entering male-dominated occupations. As long as girls constitute a small minority of apprentices, they are likely to need extra support even once they are enrolled.

Finally, there is a need outside the apprenticeship system for measures to encourage girls and young women to enter apprentice training in traditionally male-dominated trade areas.

The Australian authorities should support guidance and counselling activities in secondary schools, TAFE, and in the Commonwealth Employment Service and state-level apprenticeship that encourage girls and young women to enter traditionally male fields.

As with other areas of training and higher education, interventions to increase female participation in non-traditional areas require extra effort to compensate for tradition and social pressures. Such extra efforts should intervene well before girls leave secondary education. The points of access to the apprenticeship system should be especially sensitive to the need of females for extra encouragement to enter male-dominated fields.

Aside from encouraging girls to enter traditionally male apprenticeship programmes, the Australian authorities also need to consider whether certain occupations now dominated by females should be apprenticeable occupations. Of the eight trade areas usually designated by state apprenticeship authorities, only two – hairdressing and food service – have appreciable numbers of females working in them. In one state (national figures on female enrolments in apprenticeship are unavailable), 91 per cent of all female apprentices were in just one trade area: hairdressing. That is a pattern consistent with the pattern of occupation by sex found in apprenticeship programmes in the other states as well.

The examiners recommend that state and Commonwealth authorities evaluate the skill requirements of certain traditionally female occupations to determine whether apprenticeship would be an appropriate vehicle for preparing persons entering those occupations.

The fact that only one female-dominated occupation is covered by apprenticeship training may reflect some degree of prejudice that tends to place a low value on the skill content of occupations that are filled mostly by women. But this also probably reflects the general rigidity of the apprenticeship system in introducing new trades and, in particular, adapting to changes in skill requirements brought on by technological change.

Deficiencies in the Quality of Apprenticeship Training

Not only is apprenticeship severely deficient with respect to whom it serves, but it is also deficient with respect to how well it trains and how cost-effective it is. Apprenticeship has been the subject of intense criticism in Australia, on grounds including that the training provided is too narrow, too long, and unable to adapt to changing skill requirements. Training provided on the job has been criticised for becoming too specialised, providing fewer skills that are readily transferable from one job to another, and interfering with the acquisition of a broad base of competences. But there is also evidence that the state and Commonwealth authorities concerned, for a variety of reasons, are reluctant to approve apprenticeships in new occupational areas[8]. Because of inadequacies in the system, it is charged that there are high wastage rates and that Australia must depend on immigration programmes to acquire large numbers of skilled workers[9].

Over time, the apprenticeship system has responded to pressure for change. The most significant changes appear to have been in the arrangements to concentrate the classroom-based component for training. This has been accomplished through pre-apprenticeship programmes and "block release". The pre-apprenticeship programmes provide up to a year of courses which tend to reduce the need for subsequent training release time. The block release programmes concentrate the one-day-a-week release time for training into blocks of time ranging from one week to six months, that may be taken any time through the apprenticeship.

These changes have made apprenticeship easier to manage for employers (by reducing intermittent release time) and young people living in rural areas (by eliminating the need to travel to training every week). They have also improved utilisation of TAFE resources and added coherence to the classroom component of training. But there is no evidence about the impact these changes have had on the skill acquisition of apprentices.

The examiners still find need for changes in apprenticeship, as well as better understanding of the consequences of some past changes.

There is a need for greater attention in apprenticeship training to broad generic skills or families of skills, to increasing the adaptability of apprentices to changing skill requirements, and to greater use of standards in the evaluation of their competences.

Commonwealth and state authorities should take steps to assure that apprenticeship maximises training in general skills that are transferable from job to job or firm to firm, and training that will equip apprentices to function in different kinds of work settings and facilitate retraining when it is necessary. To accomplish this, authorities should encourage identification of generic skills and families of skills and support extension of broad-based training such as the family-of-skills pre-employment programmes in use in Queensland and South Australia. The examiners are aware of the difficulty and uncertainty in pinpointing generic skills and providing training in them that also fully prepares a young person for a job. But the examiners see a generic skills approach as being essential to the process of equipping young people not just for immediate employment, but to increase their personal ability to adapt to changes in occupational specialities and skill requirements that accompany the inevitable structural changes in the Australian economy.

That portion of apprenticeship training that is provided at the work site needs to be watched more closely. With the wider use of pre-apprenticeship and block release training, there is a danger of training in the workplace becoming too isolated from that in the classroom. Moreover, there is clear evidence that some training provided on the job is too narrow to be used in other firms or even in other jobs in the same firm. This is particularly true for apprentices working for small enterprises.

There need to be standards for evaluating the competences of apprentices. The examiners are not suggesting standardisation of all apprenticeship training. But there is a need to be assured that apprentices within a given trade area have indeed learned certain core skills.

Commonwealth and state apprenticeship authorities should determine whether there is a need for more flexibility in designating new trade areas.

As high technology leads to the disappearance of some jobs and the creation of others, it is vitally important that Australian authorities take steps to assure that training resources adapt to changing skill requirements. Since apprenticeship arrangements have been criticised for years in Australia for being incapable of dealing with change, authorities should find out whether reforms could make the system more adaptable. If greater adaptability is not possible, apprenticeship should be reserved for traditional trades (with training being reduced in those areas where occupations are becoming obsolete), and alternative standards-based arrangements should be developed to provide training for new occupational areas.

Regardless of other changes that may be made in apprenticeship, authorities should assure that it is compatible with the requirements of the Youth Entitlement.

One of the objectives of the Youth Entitlement is to assure that young people are adequately equipped to plan and pursue their careers. Authorities should take steps to assure that either apprenticeship or pre-apprenticeship activities include such preparation for those young people going directly into apprenticeship after compulsory schooling.

Fluctuations in Apprenticeship Levels

Another weakness of apprenticeship in Australia is its vulnerability to changing economic conditions. Since the onset of the current recession, the number of new apprentices enrolled each year has dropped 30 per cent to a level of 36 000, about 20 per cent below the level of training that the Commonwealth estimates is needed in the Australian economy.

The current recession has driven home the fact that when employers are pressed to cut costs, apprenticeship is expendable. This may be due in part to employers' dissatisfaction with the quality of apprenticeship training. If so, the drop in apprenticeships may not reflect a net drop in training but, instead, a reallocation by employers of their resources to other modes of training. But, considering the timing and the size of the drop in apprenticeship intakes, it seems likely that costs are the major contributing factor. The Australian authorities so far have tried to shelter apprenticeship from economic shocks by reducing the costs to employers through such programmes as the Commonwealth Rebate for Apprenticeship Full-time Training (CRAFT), Special Apprenticeship Assistance, and Group Apprenticeship schemes. The continuing decline in intakes indicates that these measures are not enough to insulate apprenticeship training levels from fluctuations in economic conditions. More should be done.

A three-part strategy is needed to improve the economic viability of apprenticeship.

i) *Redefine the way apprenticeship costs are treated by employers*

Apprenticeship training is a form of investment. The initial costs produce a stream of benefits over time in the form of more productive workers. Yet, currently, apprenticeship costs are treated as variable costs for employers, like the costs of employing a worker. During any lull in economic activity when employers need to cut variable costs to stay competitive, apprenticeship training inevitably suffers. Authorities should consider permitting employers to treat apprenticeship costs like other investment costs.

Another approach is to impose a "training levy" refunding it to those employers who engage apprentices. This kind of levy was introduced in the United Kingdom and proposed in Germany. It was ended in the United Kingdom in 1983 and never enacted in Germany, in both cases because of strong resistance on the part of employers. The levy adopted in the United Kingdom was never formally evaluated to determine if it increased the amount of training done. But though a levy may not increase the amount of training, it may serve to redistribute the burden of costs more evenly between those firms that train and those that do not.

ii) *Reduce the overall obligation apprenticeship imposes on small enterprises.*

Apprenticeship imposes a long-term obligation on employers, an obligation that small employers shy away from, especially during times when business prospects are uncertain. Group apprenticeship schemes are one way of reducing this obligation. These schemes act as nominal employers of apprentices, "leasing" them to individual employers. The schemes cancel, to some extent, the training costs associated with apprenticeship by not requiring individual employers to indenture apprentices for a long period of time. They have the added benefit of giving trainees the opportunity to work with a greater variety of employers by including those employers who otherwise could not afford the full costs or the time commitment for apprenticeship training.

iii) *Evaluate the need for redistributing between government and employers the burden of supporting apprenticeship*

Apprenticeship can be a mutually beneficial training arrangement with regard to government and employer. In return for government support, employers provide training that increases the productivity of an apprentice, but also provides skills that can be transported to other jobs. To the extent the allocation of costs of apprenticeship between government and employers is an issue, any such decision should be based as much as possible on an analysis of how much training benefits the employers providing it, and how much society at large. As a broad criterion in any decision to reallocate costs, government should underwrite the costs of general training that is indeed transportable to other employers, while the employer should pay for specific training that is usable only in his firm. In practical terms, it may be most feasible to stipulate that general training is limited to that provided in an institutional setting, unless firms can demonstrate through a competence documentation process that certain skills gained on the job are at a sufficiently high level and are sufficiently adaptable to other work settings to be considered general training.

Whatever Australian authorities do, the long-term goal should be to assure a predictable stream of apprenticeship intakes. The size and composition of that stream should reflect projected long-term skill requirements, and not simply the level of apprenticeship training that is affordable in the short run.

Informal Work-based Training

Uncredentialed and unsubsidised training provided on the job may be perhaps Australia's largest training resource. Most Australians enter the workforce without a recognised skill credential, find a job, and are trained over a period of time while they work. The examiners did not have the opportunity to study job-based training and it is virtually impossible to get definitive data on exactly how many people are trained that way, the relative importance of that training in different occupational areas, and its value. Two things are quite clear regarding job-based training, though: it is large and is an important skill training resource, particularly for young workers, the ones most likely to be starting a job with no skill credentials and no prior work experience; those who receive training in it have little to show for it with respect to recognisable, credentialed skills.

Since the available evidence does indicate that job-based training is an important resource for many Australians, national authorities should take certain steps to support it and to add structure to the "system" by ensuring that competences gained by workers on the job are evaluated on the basis of standards, and credentialed.

Presently, apprenticeship is the main vehicle for government support of job-based training. But since it is a highly structured and formalized mechanism, it might be useful to develop a more flexible format that strikes a compromise between apprenticeship and the way in which job-based training is practised now.

Wider use of sanctioned training contracts to establish cadetships or traineeships (like those possible in New South Wales) might be one approach to adding structure to job-based training. Contracts would be for training much shorter than traditional apprenticeship arrangements and would not impose the long-term commitment on employers, but could set certain training objectives to be met by employers. In return, employers might be paid a rebate to cover direct training costs or release time for trainees to attend classroom-based instruction. Trainee competences would be evaluated on the basis of standards, possibly developed by TAFE. The latter, or some joint employer-union labour market body, could assume responsibility for evaluating competences and awarding certificates. The administrative mechanism sanctioning training contracts and making payments to employers could also be used as a basis for collecting more information on job-based training.

Regardless of what arrangements are made to formalize job-based training, there is a need for standards for evaluating occupational skill competences. This has been discussed already with regard to TAFE. Standards and competence assessment techniques that are developed in TAFE might also be used to assess competences gained in training on the job. In fact, skills assessment and credentialing might be carried out by TAFE institutions with assistance from employers and unions, as a way of giving employers and workers a credible basis for measuring worker qualifications gained in job-based training or elsewhere.

Whatever is done regarding job-based training, Australian authorities need to pay attention to how the financial burden for job-based training is shared between government and employers.

An important factor to consider in deciding what training is appropriately publicly supported and what is not, is who such training benefits: just the employers providing it, or other employers and society at large?

A great deal of the training that workers might receive on the job is likely to be geared to specific tasks and responsibilities of particular employers. It does not provide the kind of skills that are readily transferable to another job or another employer. Consequently, while making workers more productive on a specific job, such training does little to improve their skills in the eyes of other employers. But at least some training provided on the job, especially that provided to young people with no previous work experience or occupational skills, is transferable to other jobs with other employers. This training improves competences of workers in ways that benefit not just the employer providing it, but other employers seeking those skills and the workers themselves. Because of the greater welfare provided by more general training, whatever public support is provided for job-based training should be targeted on it by specifying general skills in training contracts.

In establishing policies regarding job-based training, the Australian authorities should take care that such policies do not undermine more structured arrangements, particularly TAFE and apprenticeship. Job-based training is inherently difficult to get information on, let alone manage as a policy intervention. Improvements that might be made in these respects are likely to be only marginal. Therefore, in the ongoing debate about how to provide adequate skill training in Australia, it is important to keep the main focus on the established institutional arrangements.

Higher Education

The examiners' greatest concern with regard to higher education was with the question of equity, not the question of overall enrolment levels. Participation in tertiary education in Australia is generally in line with the experience of other OECD countries, both with respect to current participation rates and past trends (see Tables 9 and 10). However, Australian authorities are concerned about the apparent decline in interest among young people in higher education, reflected in participation rates that have fallen steadily over the last several years (though a slight increase in 1983 may signal the end of the decline). The examiners believe the concerns *may* have some basis, if only because the uncertain value of TAFE training raises questions about whether Australia will be able to meet its future requirements for more educated workers. But the question of what would be an appropriate participation rate of young people in higher education is one beyond the scope of this report. It requires, at a minimum, more detailed occupational forecasts and estimates of skill requirements and projections on immigration flows, for example. What the examiners did consider feasible to consider and important, however, was the question of who increasing higher enrolments might include.

Table 9. **Comparative Measures of Participation in Higher Education**[a] (1981)

Country	Proportion of a generation entering higher education – 1981[a] (Per thousand)	Enrolment rates in higher education (%)
Australia	368	24.9
Denmark	327[b]	28.1
France	340	25.1
Germany	195[b]	21.4
Japan	358	30.7
Sweden	251[c]	36.8
United Kingdom	285[d]	18.7
United States	617	56.7

a) *Source:* OECD educational statistics
b) 1980.
c) 1979.
d) Universities full-time and advanced further education; full-time and part-time for Wales and England only; includes courses of university and non-university level.

Table 10. **Proportion of a Generation Entering Higher Education: Trend 1965-1981**
Per thousand

	1965	1970	1975	1976	1977	1978	1979	1980	1981
Germany	122	153	195	194	185	186	184	195	
Australia			364		349	364	356	360	368
Denmark			353	345	303[a]	300[a]	290[a]	327	
United States	431	551	600	559	573	573	591	608	617
France			275	281	290	289	319	318	340
Japan	144	243	390	376	376	382	370	365	358
United Kingdom		199		274	280	286	285		
Sweden	134	229	248	266 //	228	243	251		

a) Without pre-primary teacher training.
// Indicates a change of classification.

In contrast, the question of *who* enrolls in tertiary education is important because of the present pattern of inequities. The examiners were especially concerned about two problems regarding access and participation in higher education:

i) The unequal access that less advantaged groups of young people have to tertiary education; and
ii) The under-representation of females in certain courses of study.

These two problems and possible remedies are discussed below. Unless these two problems are addressed, Australian authorities run the risk of having a higher education system that serves students according to income, socio-economic status and gender, and ultimately contributes to a workforce of professionals and non-professionals, stratified along class lines.

Access of Disadvantaged Young People

In Australia, as in virtually every other OECD country, young people from lower-income families and whose parents have only limited education are under-represented in higher education. The examiners think their participation in higher education should be greater because it is one of the best vehicles for upward mobility and increased earnings. It is also of special concern to the examiners because the Australian authorities have already done so much to try to equalise higher education opportunities.

In order to improve access to higher education, the Commonwealth, under the Labour Government in the 1970s, eliminated tuition charges and fees for attendance at all universities and colleges of advanced education. It was hoped that this, combined with the education assistance allowances, would further mitigate the effects of family income as a determinant of participation in higher education. In fact, the socio-economic profile of the higher enrolment has hardly changed at all. Graduates of non-government schools, the schools that typically enroll more advantaged students, are over-represented in colleges of advanced education, and heavily over-represented in universities, which are the entry point to professional jobs. Graduates of government schools are under-represented in both.

A recent review of participation by different socio-economic groups in higher education implies that strategies for equalising access require intervention well before the point at which young people enter universities and colleges of advanced education. The conclusion of the authors is that family background exerts its greatest influence in determining what secondary school a young person will attend (government, Catholic, or other non-government) and what courses he or she will take while attending school. These factors in turn are the ones most important in determining whether young people complete secondary school and are prepared appropriately for continuing in higher education. Students completing year twelve of secondary schooling have fairly equal chances for continuing on to higher education, irrespective of socio-economic status[10].

At a minimum, the implication is that a strategy for equalising participation in higher education must include measures at the secondary level. Evidence in other countries where disadvantaged students are more likely to participate in post-secondary studies also indicates a need for continued intervention beyond the point of enrolment in tertiary education.

In order to increase participation of disadvantaged students in higher education, the Australian authorities should intervene not just at the higher level, but also at the secondary level and in TAFE; i) at the secondary level to increase the number of disadvantaged young people completing the final year and going on to tertiary education; ii) in TAFE to develop courses of study that would provide an alternative route of access to higher education; iii) at the higher level to facilitate admission and to assure retention.

Hopefully, secondary school reforms to increase retention through year twelve will increase participation by lower socio-economic status students in tertiary education. But additional counselling and guidance may be needed to compensate for a lack of strong family support for enrolment in higher education. In light of the success of TAFE institutions in attracting early school-leavers, TAFE and higher education authorities should consult on developing in TAFE alternative courses of preparation for college and university education. Such alternatives could be designed for those young people who have difficulty in the more traditional education climate of secondary schools, and for those young people who, having decided earlier to pursue technical skill training, decide to pursue higher education.

As is recommended earlier, in order to make upper secondary education more attractive, schools need to avoid having higher education entrance requirements dictate the content of secondary curricula and the student assessment practices. But, at the same time, colleges and universities need to be more flexible in evaluating the ability of applicants. Increased flexibility should take two forms. First, there is apparently a need for more flexibile criteria for evaluating ability. These might include taking into account the limited language skills of first- and second-generation immigrants from non-English speaking countries, as well as the fact that, because secondary education has evidently alienated many young people, secondary school records are not likely to be a valid indicator of ability. Second, higher education institutions should probably reassess entry requirements to determine whether broader secondary education – especially at the upper secondary level – might not be desirable. None of this is to suggest lowering standards or admitting young people who are not likely to be able to benefit from higher education. Rather, flexibility is encouraged to assure better that ability is evaluated on the basis of something other than how well young people can get on in a secondary school setting that has in the past demonstrated itself to be suspect in serving large numbers of disadvantaged young people.

Finally, if tertiary institutions do succeed in attracting more disadvantaged students, these are likely to need extra help, including remedial assistance, counselling, and possibly supplemental income support, if they are to stay enrolled.

Enrolment Patterns of Girls and Young Women

The examiners are concerned that enrolment patterns at the higher level change in order to achieve equality of opportunity for females in the labour market. Presently, though there have been steady improvements over recent years, girls and young women enrolled in higher education in Australia still are more likely than their male counterparts to be over-represented in the fine arts, liberal arts, education and other courses of study leading to lower-paying, lower-status jobs. In this respect, higher education enrolment patterns contribute to patterns in the labour market of occupational segregation by sex, and lower earnings for women.

Achieving more balanced enrolments for females in higher education will also require strategies at the secondary level as well as the higher level. The segregation by sex in higher enrolment patterns is influenced by the kind of preparation girls have had in secondary school, and also by decisions they make once they enroll in higher education. To the extent they do not take the courses in secondary education that are required for entrance into sciences, math and engineering, female students have certain opportunities foreclosed from the time they enter colleges and universities. But others, even when they have the latitude to enroll in courses of studies that are male-dominated, choose not to. Ultimately, in both cases, the choices of males and females are heavily influenced by tradition, parental pressure and social pressure.

In order to achieve more balanced enrolments for females in higher education, Australian authorities should intervene at the secondary level, not just at the tertiary level.

At the secondary level, counselling and other interventions to break down sex-role stereotyping need to be geared to encouraging girls to take more science and math courses. This will give them the flexibility to enter more of the professional streams that are now male-dominated. At the same time, colleges and universities need to provide encouragement through counselling and guidance activities to assure that, once females are admitted, more indeed do enroll in sciences, math, engineering, and other courses of studies leading to higher-status, higher-paid jobs.

Conclusions

The skills required of Australians entering the labour market are changing as a result of structural shifts induced in the economy by new technology, changing patterns of international trade, and changing consumer tastes. Jobs that have traditionally required only limited education, and little in the way of occupational skills beyond those that could be learned on the jobs, are disappearing. Employment growth is in the occupational areas requiring higher levels of education and technical, para-professional, and professional training. These structural changes are downgrading the importance of manual skills and physical strength as factors determining employability and upgrading the importance of formal education and training. These changes require the education and training institutions to change what they are doing.

But other developments in Australia are dictating change, as well. A new social climate and different social priorities require that Australian authorities make sure that access to various education and training institutions is open to all; in particular, this means assuring better access for females and disadvantaged youth. These considerations are important because education and training arrangements in the past have reinforced sex-role stereotyping in the preparation of girls and young women for work, and contributed to occupational segregation by sex. Disadvantaged youth have not had their educational and training needs met, nor the social needs that may interfere with their participation in education and training. Changes are needed in the content of what education and training institutions do, and in whom they serve. The bulk of the changes needs to come in existing institutions: secondary schools, tertiary institutions, TAFE, and the apprenticeship system. The transition requires much more than add-on programmes that influence at the margin while leaving basic structures intact. This will require an active role by state as well as Commonwealth government.

If changes are not made in the content of what education and training institutions do, and if the expected structural changes do occur, the Australian economy could encounter skill bottlenecks that will interfere with its adaptability and competitive posture. If changes are not made to assure more equal access to education and training opportunities, women and certain workers with limited education and skills will be isolated increasingly from the better jobs, as part of a permanent second-class workforce.

NOTES AND REFERENCES

1. Office of the Status of Women, *Meeting Young Women's Needs* (Canberra: November 1983).
2. Treasurer of the Commonwealth of Australia and the Minister of Finance, *Budget Statements 1983-84* (Australian Government Publishing Service, Canberra: 1983), p. 89.
3. Department of Employment and Industrial Relations, *Employment Prospects by Industry and Occupation: A Labour Market Analysis* (Australian Government Publishing Service, Canberra: 1983).
4. Committee of Inquiry into Education and Training, *Education, Training and Employment: Vol. I* (Australian Government Publishing Service, Canberra: 1979), pp. 327-28.
5. See Chris Hayes et al., *Training for Skill Ownership: Learning to Take It with You* (Institute for Manpower Studies, Brighton: 1983).
6. See Remediation and Training Institute, *Comprehensive Competencies Program* (Remediation and Training Institute, Alexandria, Virginia: 1983) and documentation on Job Corps and the Job Corps Educational Improvement Effort available from National Job Corps Office, Employment and Training Administration, U.S. Department of Labor, Washington, D.C. 20213.
7. Women's Bureau, "Gender Wage Differentials in Australia" (Department of Employment and Industrial Relations, Canberra: August 1983).
8. L. Ridell, "Discussion Paper on Apprenticeship and Training: Current Developments and Future Options" (New South Wales, Department of Technical and Further Education, October 1983).
9. See, for example, Committee of Inquiry into Education and Training, *Education, Training and Employment, Vol. I* (Australian Government Publishing Service, Canberra: 1979), pp. 356-364.
10. D.S. Anderson and A.E. Vervoorn, *Access to Privilege: Patterns of Participation in Australian Post-secondary Education* (A.N.U. Press, Canberra: 1983).

Chapter 4

INCOME SUPPORT

Income support for young people is the single most controversial issue in the debate on youth policies in Australia. Though virtually everyone – government authorities, parents, young people and youth advocates – agrees that the current arrangements are in large measure complex, inconsistent and inequitable and create perverse incentives, there is no consensus over how to make improvements. The "gridlock" created by the present collection of arrangements means that every proposed "improvement" introduces a new complexity or inequity, reorders incentives, or is intolerably expensive; every proposed change makes new winners and losers.

But the examiners found that the struggle to make sense of the income support measures for young people is, in some respects, a misdirected search for technical solutions to political problems. The controversy over income support for young people seems to swirl around technical questions of how to "rationalise" the various arrangements, without first fully recognising what purpose a rationalised income support system for young people might serve. Two questions in particular need to be answered to establish a basis for discussing these measures, but they require fundamentally political answers:

– What should be the role of youth income support measures in reducing poverty and economic inequality?
– What level of resources will be made available for income support measures?

These questions need to be answered before more technical questions of support level, grant consolidation, income tests and relative incentives can be dealt with finally, because answers to the technical questions hinge in large part on the larger political decisions. The discussion below examines the underlying political questions first and considers their implications for the more technical issues that follow.

Issues at the Foundation of an Income Support System for Youth

The two issues considered below are not the only ones reflecting what are essentially political considerations, but they seem to be the most important ones. They are at the heart of the more significant technical problems, and if left unresolved, threaten to undermine the solutions that are finally put forth.

Poverty and Socio-economic Inequality

Before the Australian authorities launch an ambitious income support scheme for young people, they need to consider whether there is a more general problem of poverty and income inequality in Australia. This is important because no matter what improvements are made in education and training arrangements, young people from poor families are less likely to benefit unless their education and training choices are truly not dependent on short-term financial considerations. The current arrangements make it advantageous (if not necessary) for young people from low-income families to choose employment (or even unemployment) in order to contribute to their family income. In light of the growing importance of education and training, any new income support provisions need to make education and training more attractive than unemployment at least, and possibly more attractive than employment for low-income youth. Otherwise, those youth, responding to immediate financial needs of their families, may never get the education and training they need to be able to break out of an employment cycle alternating between low-paying jobs for unskilled workers and unemployment.

To the extent that there is a larger problem of poverty and socio-economic inequality, authorities need to take steps to assure that any youth schemes are consistent and compatible with other income support measures. If they do not, any new scheme may create new anomalies or force youths from low-income families into economic independence at a cost to the financial well-being of their families.

In their work, the examiners found evidence of persistent conditions of socio-economic inequality as well as evidence for concern about substantial and possibly increasing poverty for some[1]. From the late 1960s through the later 1970s, there was improvement in equality with the two highest deciles' share of income declining slightly and the two lowest gaining, most dramatically between 1973-74 and 1978-79 when their share rose from 1.7 to 2.7 per cent. But the trend turned around in the period from 1978-79 to 1981-82, when the two highest deciles' share edged up a point, while the two lowest and the six lowest edged down[2]. While Australia in the past has compared favourably with other OECD countries with respect to equality of income distribution[3], the recent deterioration may have changed that, though more current comparative data are not available.

The shifts in relative income shares are worrisome for their possible negative effects on income inequality and relative poverty. But there is also evidence of a danger of increasing absolute poverty because of the increases in the relative size of two population groups prone to poverty: single mothers and elderly persons. Divorce and separation in Australia are leaving increasingly large numbers of families headed by women. This is creating a growing class of persons in need of aid. Women, as a group, are less likely to be employed than males [41 per cent for females over 15 years compared to 70 per cent for males in May 1984[4]], and those who are employed are likely to earn less [the mean wage and salary annual income for females is 66 per cent of that for males in August 1983[5]]. Similarly, the proportion of elderly people in the total population is increasing. Between 1971 and 1981, the absolute size of the population 65 years and over grew by a third, far outpacing the growth of other groups; while their share of the total population increased from 8.3 to 9.7 per cent, the share for 15-64 year-olds increased from 63.0 to 65.3 per cent, and the share for those under 15 years decreased from 28.7 to 25 per cent[6].

The increasing growth in the numbers of older persons, single parents (mostly women), and unemployed were the three biggest components in the increase in pensioners and beneficiaries in Australia, whose share of the total population rose from 10.5 per cent in 1973 to 21.3 per cent in 1983. While improving economic conditions will reduce the number of unemployed persons, it will have no effect on the number of older persons and sole parents. Though better economic conditions are likely to improve the economic fortunes of some of them, they are likely to remain a large and growing group, prone to poverty.

Certainly, none of this establishes definitively that older persons and single parents should be given highest priority in any changes in income support arrangements. There are other groups in the population, including the young, who also run a risk of being economically disadvantaged. It is also not clear that there is an underlying secular trend towards greater income inequality or poverty in Australia. In fact, much of what is happening might be the consequences of the recession following the second oil shock falling especially heavily on lower-income workers. Nevertheless, there appears to be a growing problem of socio-economic inequality, and at least a threat of increasing poverty in Australia. Although an inquiry into socio-economic inequality and poverty is beyond the terms of reference of this review, the examiners found little evidence that the discussions of youth income support or proposals for changing the current arrangements were in any way taking account of the larger problem of socio-economic inequality and poverty. If this larger context is ignored, there is a danger that any serious overhaul of youth income support programmes will be dismissed as being too narrow, or if it is adopted, it will create new problems.

This larger context complicates the challenge of making sense of the income support arrangements now serving young people. Many of the complexities, inequities, unbalanced incentives, and perhaps costs of the current income support arrangements for young people reflect the fact that they evolved independently of one another (as in other countries). Young people may receive three principal different kinds of income support: social security and unemployment benefits, educational assistance, and training assistance. The three categories are administered by three separate departments. The basis for the different kinds of aid varies, some being based on legislation and regulations subject to legislative review, others on regulations subject to no review, and some are based just on departmental policy.

The administrative arrangements for income support in Australia, complicated as they are, are not unlike those found in other countries. They reflect the fact that income support is a government function that overlaps and affects other functional areas, such as education and employment. The inherent overlap may contribute to a splintered policy-making process when income support arrangements for education, for example, are subordinate to a larger process of developing education policy. It certainly makes it difficult to orchestrate various arrangements spread among different departments. But these difficulties notwithstanding, there is room for improvement.

The examiners find the existing arrangements to be plagued by incompatibilities because too little attention has been given to their collective impact on a large group of clients: young people. While various aid initiatives in each of the categories were launched at different times to serve different purposes, there was no effective mechanism for overseeing the impact of the measures taken together and adjusting them accordingly. This contributed to the situation in which young people could, for example, receive more money for leaving secondary school early and enrolling in TAFE, or even more money for entering the labour market without skills and either finding low-paid employment or receiving unemployment benefits for doing nothing, or engaging in job search that is not likely to be productive because of skill mismatches or an absence of jobs. The examiners are concerned that Australian authorities, in succeeding now in making narrow improvements in income support measures for young people, run the risk once again of making it more difficult to deal with a larger problem of poverty and socio-economic inequality.

In developing new income support schemes for young people, the Australian authorities need to consider the problems facing youth in the context of more general conditions of poverty and economic inequality, and need to assure that any new initiatives are not inconsistent or incompatible with other income support schemes. In particular, Australian authorities need to consider the redistributional effects of proposed alternatives to determine whether they might aggravate income inequality.

Resources

The issue of resources is germane to all aspects of youth policies under consideration in Australia, but probably figures most prominently in the income support question. Income support provisions are already a major component of Commonwealth outlays on youth. Unlike some of the education and training activities where policies might be changed by reallocating existing resources to new functions, shifts in income support policies can have major cost implications. In meetings and in material provided to the examiners, the Australian authorities stressed resource constraints repeatedly and emphasized the importance of developing youth policies based on reallocating existing resources for young people rather than incurring new expenditures. This mandate may be difficult to follow, at least with respect to income support measures. The examiners have two reasons for at least questioning the wisdom of the proposition that changes in policies should be accomplished with no or few net new costs.

i) *While reallocation of resources may not involve net new budget costs, such policies will certainly impose costs on those who lose money in the reallocation process;*

Most of the difficulties that Australian authorities face in trying to "rationalise" income support arrangements for young persons stem from the fact that there are so many provisions already in place, each with its own payment level and eligibility conditions. One way to rationalise these measures and make, for example, unemployment less attractive than full-time enrolment in vocational training is to treat the highest paying "option" as a floor and build up other provisions to that floor level (to make choices neutral with respect to benefit) or to a level above (to make certain choices financially more attractive than others). The problem with this approach is that it adds net costs to the Commonwealth budget. But the alternative, reallocating existing resources to make all choices fiscally neutral or to make some intentionally more attractive than others, also imposes costs on the persons whose benefits are reduced in order to make other choices more attractive. Australian authorities need to consider if those costs in lost income to certain individuals are equitable (and sustainable politically).

In reallocating existing resources, the Australian authorities need to be especially careful not to create a system that is biased against low-income persons. Even if relative incentives are such that education and training are more attractive then unemployment, low-income youth almost certainly will continue to be the least likely to participate. Unemployment benefits for them should not be reduced to a level below what is needed for subsistence, in order to pay for higher education and training benefits.

ii) *Australia can, in fact, probably afford some net new costs, if there is the political will to approve them;*

The examiners certainly understand the hazards of increasing public revenues and outlays and the importance of improving the efficiency and cost-effectiveness of public sector spending. But they conclude that if, in fact, a reasonable scheme for rationalising income support for youth can be devised, some net increases in income support can be sustained. Resource constraints, tight as they may be in Australia, are not as tight as those faced in other OECD countries. Government expenditures take up a smaller share of GDP than they do in most other OECD countries. Moreover, tax effort, when measured as the share of GDP taken up in Australia by tax receipts, was in 1982 the seventh lowest of the 23 countries in the OECD area[7].

The decision of whether to dedicate more resources to solving those problems is very much a decision about *priorities*. What other countries do with respect to tax burdens is not likely to be a very compelling political argument in Australia. Rather, the decisive factor is likely to be how seriously the Australian authorities and the public at large take the problems facing young people in Australia.

Australian authorities should carefully evaluate their various income support options on the basis of net cost, to see how much "low-cost" options actually hide costs by shifting them from government to society at large, from the short term to the long term, or from youth income-support budget categories to budget categories for other social services.

In considering the costs of various income support options, authorities should consider more than simply net changes in budget resources for youth in the next fiscal year. Evaluating costs strictly on the basis of those reflected in the Commonwealth budget is misleading and may contribute to false economies. There are social costs to certain "no-cost" policies that, for example, do not provide sufficient short-term incentives to disadvantaged youth to enroll in further education or training. Such costs include lower productivity, lower earnings and a higher likelihood of unemployment. These, in turn, can lead to greater costs for long-term social dependence, to say nothing of the costs to individuals of wasted ability, and less fulfillment in their working and personal lives. These social costs are far harder to evaluate than budget costs. They are incurred over a longer period and some, particularly the less tangible, individual costs are hard to value in dollar terms. But they are just as real and while the individual costs might be cynically dismissed because they are not paid by the government, social dependence costs are. Ignoring those in the short run risks increasing the public obligation in the long run.

The Challenge to Rationalising Income Support for Youth in Australia

Choices about the equity goals and resource level of income support provisions for young people will be most important in determining the scale of the impact of changes. The more involved details of rationalisation will depend upon the choice of particular policy objectives and constraints. In the following discussion, the examiners indicate what seem to be the most important objectives and constraints, and then consider changes that might be made in the existing arrangements.

Objectives and Constraints

After reviewing material and meeting with the various persons inside and outside government, the examiners conclude that the principal objective of income support measures for young people should be to enable them to choose their options subject to certain constraints, according to what their preferences are, by eliminating as much as possible short-term financial factors as determinants of choice.

Young people of school-leaving age can choose, in principle, among six different courses of action:

i) Continue in secondary school in order to be awarded a higher school certificate and, possibly, continue on to higher education;
ii) Enter an apprenticeship;
iii) Enroll in institution-based technical/vocational training;
iv) Enroll in non-vocationally oriented training;

v) Enter the labour force; or

vi) Pursue personal interests such as travel, hobbies – activities that are outside the labour force and not explicitly geared to preparing young people for later employment.

As a rule, employment, if it can be found, is the most lucrative activity in the short run. But with the prospects for high youth unemployment continuing, the employment option is less promising (for the time being), especially for young people trying to start stable careers. As employment declines as a viable option, it becomes more feasible to fashion income support arrangements that, as a first step, neutralise the relative short-term financial advantage of the remaining choices. This can be done most directly by assuring that the income support payments are roughly equal, regardless of what activity a young person pursues.

However, it is not politically or fiscally feasible nor is it effective public policy to develop a completely unconstrained income support scheme for young people. As the discussion in the preceding section indicates, such a scheme cannot be developed or operated in a vacuum, isolated from other income support and larger social policies. Constraints are needed to assure that youth income support measures are consistent and compatible with other policies.

Youth income support measures should be developed subject to three constraints in particular:

i) *To reward most those activities that will most effectively serve the general welfare*

Income support measures for young people, while permitting genuine choices as much as possible, should reward those activities by young people that will most help the general welfare. It might be argued that, ideally, state-provided income support should maximise individual choice, not favouring one over another. Indeed, if Australian authorities were confident of long-term labour and skill surpluses and were satisfied that there was opportunity for real socio-economic mobility, they might be well-advised to subsidise any activity that would keep young people out of the labour market – and lower their unemployment rates.

But as Chapters 2 and 3 indicate, the examiners do not believe that Australia can afford the luxury of subsidising activity that does not contribute to improving socio-economic equality or the education and vocational skill level of the labour force. In supporting alternatives to work and unemployment, income support measures must do more than simply reduce youth unemployment rates. They should contribute positively to the general welfare.

Income support measures should be designed to make sure that those choices that will help the general welfare most – namely education and vocational training – yield the highest short-term financial gain. It might be added that the kind of improvements in education and training arrangements discussed in Chapter 3 will presumably improve the long-term gains of such activities enough so that the differential income support benefit for these choices would not need to be too high or might even be neutral.

ii) *To reinforce policies for improving socio-economic equality;*

Income support policies should contribute to socio-economic equality by taking into account exactly whose choices are expanded, and the redistributional impacts of income support payments. Income support schemes for young people should be managed so that, together with changes in education and training policies, they increase the proportion of young persons from disadvantaged backgrounds participating in education and training.

Ironically, the current high youth unemployment presents Australian authorities with a rare opportunity for using income support policies for improving socio-economic equality, as well as enhancing the skill level of the labour force. During a period of limited employment opportunities, it is less expensive to raise the short-run financial pay-off of education and training activities relative to unemployment benefits or employment because the present unemployment benefits are low and employment opportunities are so limited. If the short-run pay-off of education and training is higher than the other options, it will help increase the education and training participation rates of those young people who, in better socio-economic times, would choose employment for immediate income because they and their families are financially hard pressed. Essentially then, the current employment climate for young people reduces the "opportunity cost" of foregoing immediate employment for the sake of training or education. This would improve income equality over the long run by increasing education attainment and skill acquisition among those groups who could not afford it in the past, and who were relegated to lower-paying jobs as adults. When employment opportunities are non-existent or limited, income support measures obviously have the greatest incentive effects on those with the lowest income. But the incentive effects must be complemented by the kind of programmatic measures discussed in Chapter 3 if these young people are to enter and succeed in education and training.

But aside from improving socio-economic equality over the long term, income support measures should be designed so that at the margin their redistributional effects favour those at the lower end of the income distribution. One way of doing that would be to assure that young people from disadvantaged backgrounds are well represented in those activities that are rewarded best. But if, for example, there is any lesson to be drawn from the higher education enrolment patterns following the elimination of tuition and fees, it is that behaviour may be hard to change. Even if an income support scheme does make enrolment in education more attractive than unemployment, it is not likely that differentials will be large enough to have major impacts on the education and training enrolments of young people who would otherwise shun those activities. And, in fact, *i)* if basic behaviour patterns do not change so that those who would have enrolled in education and training anyway are the only ones who do, and *ii)* support payment is based strictly on the choice a young person makes, then the redistributional consequences will be in the direction of greater income inequality.

One way to keep this from happening is to assure that most income support benefits are income-tested. By income-testing eligibility for some benefits for education and training, and providing benefits graduated on the basis of income, for example, it would be possible to keep participation in education and training more attractive than unemployment. At the same time this would minimise the dead weight subsidy (and perverse redistributional effects) to more advantaged students who would have participated in "preferred" activities anyway.

The examiners favour determining eligibility and benefit levels on the basis of income. This approach may be more difficult to administer than a system relying more on flat grants and a progressive income tax system to tax away benefits paid to better-off families or individuals. But they believe that a system that bases eligibility and benefit levels on income is more likely to be able to provide adequate support to those who need it. Less income-testing, more flat payments, and reliance on tax mechanisms to bring net benefits in line with need, will require at the outset payments to a larger number of beneficiaries. If the payments are to be adequate for those most in need, the overall outlays are likely to be so high as to be politically unfeasible, regardless of what the final net transfers may be. It seems more likely that there would be a high risk of benefit levels being reduced to minimise budget outlays, regardless of the increase in tax revenues that might follow.

iii) *To maximise the objectives for any given level of expenditures;*

The point of this is to stress the fact that, regardless of total level of resources for income support, the marginal effectiveness and efficiency of any arrangement in achieving the scheme's objectives within constraints is a function of design, not resource level. Though the examiners argued earlier in this chapter in favour of not deciding to limit income support resources prematurely, design is even more important. A well-designed but poorly-funded scheme can accomplish more net good than a poorly-designed, well-funded scheme.

Changing Existing Arrangements

In looking at the existing income support arrangements in the three areas of social security, education and training, the examiners have restricted their analysis to the largest schemes that are directly related to labour market, education, and training activities. These schemes taken together serve the vast majority of all young recipients, and comprise, by far, the largest share of total expenditures for young people in each of the three areas (see Table 11).

Table 11. **Principal Income Support Programmes for 15-24 Year-olds**

	Numbers assisted 30 June 1983	Expenditures 1982/83 $m
Social security income support		
Unemployment benefit	308 781	990.0
Single-parent pension[a]	45 456	255.8
Family allowance	583 270	201.8
Proportion of all social security programmes	(90%)	(89%)
Education income support		
Secondary allowance	44 430	29.0
Tertiary education assistance	70 913	170.0
Proportion of all education income assistance	(86%)	(88%)

	Number approved for assistance by 30 June 1983	
Training income support		
Transition allowance	14 113	11.4
Pre-apprenticeship	3 785	1.9
CRAFT living allowance	5 379	n.a.
Community youth support scheme	65 000	17.9
Proportion of all training income support programmes	(96%)	(89%)

a) The single-parent pension is not discussed in the analysis because its benefits and eligibility for it are independent of education and training status, and dependent on labour market status only to the extent that eligibility is means-tested.

There are four important areas of concern regarding the present income support arrangements: their incentive effects, adequacy with regard to meeting recipient needs, complexity, and the question of who should receive payments – young people or their parents.

The most important concern is the incentive effects. To the extent young people or their parents are trying to maximise their income, the current arrangements favour choices that, in

Table 12. **Best and Worst Paying Options for Typical Young Person Living at Home**

Option	Age Group 16-17	Age Group 18-19	Maximum benefits over 4 years (undiscounted)
Best	Leave school and enter TAFE or transition activity such as CYSS; receive $51/week.	Enroll in TAFE or a transition activity such as CYSS; receive $84.60/week.	Youth receives $13 321.20
Second best	Unemployment; receive $45/week.	Unemployment; receive $78.60/week.	Youth receives $12 097.20
Worst	Stay in school; receive nothing, but parents receive $20.12/week for enrolment in year 11 and 12.	Stay in year 12 of secondary school and parents receive $20.12/week.	Parents receive $2 052.24[a]
		Enter tertiary education (other than TAFE) and receive $40.58.	Youth receives $4 139.16[a]

If parents must meet the various means tests, there is no particular incentive to leave home. If they do not, a young person attending a tertiary institution could leave home and receive $22 per week more, though the parents would lose between $5.25 and $10.50 per week in family allowance for children 16-17 years of age. (The family allowance is not included in the analysis because it is the same in each case for young people living at home.)

[a] Additional payments are available in the case of students from pensioner and beneficiary families (these additional benefits do not change the order of the options).

the long term, do not improve income equality, and might not improve overall the education and skill level of the workforce.

Table 12 presents in a stylised fashion the principal options facing a typical young person living at home. As the table indicates, the current arrangements strongly discourage secondary education and favour training only slightly over idle joblessness or job search that is not necessarily likely to be productive. The "income maximising" young person's best choice is to leave school in time to establish eligibility for a transition allowance at age 16 and stay enrolled in TAFE or enter a transitional activity such as the Community Youth Support Scheme. This would not be such a bad choice if there were clear assurances that TAFE courses increased employability and skill competences substantially (see Chapter 3), or the participation in activities such as CYSS substantially improved a young person's later chance of finding employment or otherwise improved their later prospects in the labour market. In fact, the evidence on the effectiveness of these interventions is not convincing and does not seem to justify favouring participation in TAFE or labour market programmes as much as they are favoured now[8].

More disturbingly, though, the current arrangements, while making training activities marginally more attractive than straight unemployment benefits, make the latter vastly more attractive than retention in secondary school and later enrolment in tertiary education.

These are not the right incentives for creating a set of arrangements that will help improve long-term economic equality and the education and skills base of the labour force. Both economic equality and a skilled workforce depend on raising, first, the level of education, and second, the level of training, particularly among those groups that now have low levels of education and training attainment.

The relative benefit levels for different activities should be reordered to increase the immediate financial rewards for education.

If youth policies are to increase socio-economic equality over the long term, upper secondary education and subsequent tertiary education must be genuinely accessible to young people from more disadvantaged backgrounds. This requires, among other things, more balanced treatment of these options under income support measures to shift those who are now unemployed into more full-time education.

Reordering the attractiveness of benefits might be accomplished in part by reducing the attractiveness of unemployment benefits as an option.

This could be accomplished by income-testing a portion of the unemployment benefits (or providing a supplement to low-income youth) and by restricting eligibility for unemployment benefits. Australia is unique among the OECD countries in allowing virtually unrestricted access to unemployment benefits for youths as young as 16 for as long as they are unemployed. Virtually all other countries require some prior employment experience, restrict the period of benefits, or after a period of time impose education or training requirements as a condition for further eligibility. It might even be possible to defer eligibility for unemployment benefits until age 17. But more needs to be done[9].

Eligibility for unemployment beyond a certain period (to allow for job search) should depend on a young person enrolling in education or training.

While the examiners fully recognise that further education and training alone will not provide jobs in the short term, they will improve employability over the long term. Young people who cannot find employment after a reasonable period of time should enroll in training or education. There is clearly more likelihood of pay-off from that than from continued job search for a young person who is unskilled and inexperienced, and very likely to find nothing more than a dead-end job.

Of course, the key to the importance of incentive effects (and, indeed, income support arrangements in general) is "supply elasticities", the responsiveness of young people to the differing benefit levels. If the behaviour of young persons who leave school, enroll in training, or simply collect unemployment benefits is determined strictly by the level of benefits that are available for the different choices, then the incentive efforts are very important to consider. In fact, evidence would indicate that relative benefit levels are not the only determinant of behaviour, and their influence under different schemes varies for different groups. Unfortunately, the pattern varies in a way which, under the present income support arrangements, most likely contributes to socio-economic inequality.

However, economic theory and available evidence indicate that the incentive effects are likely to be more influential for low-income families for whom transfer payments of any kind make up a larger share of their total income. It is reasonable therefore to conclude that they will be more sensitive to fluctuations in benefit levels. In 1981-82, 62 per cent of those earning less than A$6 000 received at least half their income in government cash benefits. Less than 3 per cent of those earning $A6 000 or more got more than one-half their income from government cash benefits[10]. Indeed, evidence regarding upper secondary school attendance (which directly influences higher education attendance) identifies socio-economic status as the most important variable in explaining who completes it: the more advantaged the student, the more likely he or she will continue in secondary education. But higher socio-economic status, besides reflecting higher income, also reflects parental influence, social conditioning and, to an extent, peer pressure. These factors act, more so than for young people from less advantaged backgrounds, to push in the direction of more education. And they counteract the negative incentive of the lower immediate financial benefits paid for staying in secondary education.

From an equity point of view, the immediate redistributional effects of the present arrangements are ideal. Most benefits (about 84 per cent) go to persons who are following the paths that will put them eventually at the lower end of the income distribution (no further education, only some training). Moreover, education benefits are income-tested.

But because it seems likely that the incentive effects are greatest for lower-income youths, the long-term effects of the present relative incentives are to worsen economic inequality, by channelling those persons into the activities with the least long-term pay-off.

It is especially important that the relative incentives for different choices be restructured to provide more encouragement for less advantaged young people to attend secondary and tertiary education.

Less advantaged youths are the ones who seem most likely to respond to reordered incentives. They are also the ones who, with respect to socio-economic equality, are likely to benefit most from more education.

Under a system of reordered incentives, graduated incentive payments should be made available on an income-tested basis.

No matter how powerful these incentive effects may be, they alone will not determine behaviour. Many young persons who will pursue education would have continued anyway. It is not really feasible to minimise the target inefficiency of that. But it is possible to avoid redistributional effects that worsen income inequality by assuring that those who do benefit from increased benefits for education, for example, are at least economically disadvantaged.

The concern about the adequacy of income support payments for meeting recipient needs is related to the issues of incentive effects, basic fairness, and the larger issue of resources. If the Australian authorities hope, through income support schemes, to increase the participation of young people in education and training activities, they have to consider not only the relative benefit levels for different activities, but the absolute benefit level as well. If differential benefits for education do not cover the direct costs of education, the incentive effects are likely to be minimal.

Adequacy of benefits is also related to a basic issue of fairness. Are benefits for the least favoured choice – unemployment, under a revised scheme – sufficient for survival? The examiners did not have access to satisfactory data on living expenses associated with school attendance or other activities. But based on poverty line estimates[1] (which the examiners found of limited usefulness) a single person, not head of household and not in the workforce, needs A$52.80 per week to cover expenses other than housing, and A$88.50 per week to cover expenses including housing[10]. The figure for total expenses is somewhat more than the most generous benefit available, the A$84.60 transition allowance paid (at the time the poverty line was estimated) to persons 18 years and older enrolled in certain TAFE courses or certain transition activities. But obviously, even if this figure is right, adequacy also depends on how much of one's expenses one really has to cover and that depends on whether a young person is living at home, in a group setting, or completely alone.

There are two strategies for assuring that benefits are adequate in absolute terms. Evaluating true expenses on a case-by-case basis (or compromising by creating more general categories) or paying a flat benefit. The first is administratively cumbersome, and by paying different amounts to young people in different settings (living at home or alone, for example) may create incentives for young people to move from one status to another. The second is certainly more costly.

In trying to set eligibility thresholds and set benefit levels that are adequate, authorities will inevitably have to strike a balance dictated by administrative ease and cost constraints; but they should be wary of trying to eliminate complexity at the same time.

Complexity is difficult to eliminate in an income support system that attempts to be efficient, equitable, and low cost. The simplest approach should be to provide a flat grant to all young people or their parents. But that is an inefficient and inequitable approach because it does not take need into account. Income-testing improves equity and efficiency, but requires administrative machinery and can create "poverty traps" – incentives for persons to limit their income in order to retain eligibility for certain benefits. An overall scheme becomes even more complex when it pays different levels of benefits for different activities. In fact, a major drawback to the existing income support arrangements may not be just their complexity *per se,* but their lack of rationality in some respects, the fact that they do sometimes support conflicting objectives, or objectives that are not consistent with other stated public policy objectives.

Eligibility for benefits should begin at age 16. That is an arbitrary choice, but it makes some sense because it would be somewhat consistent with existing arrangements. That is the age at which eligibility for unemployment benefits begins, and it is the age at which many students begin year eleven and they become eligible for payments under the Secondary Allowance Scheme. Eligibility for benefits (except for unemployment) paid to young people as part of an overall policy for their development should probably end in their early 20s, at a time when most initial education and training would be ended.

In developing income support schemes for young people, the Australian authorities should try most of all to keep them rational and consistent rather than merely simple.

In deciding whom to pay benefits to, the Australian authorities need to balance two opposing forces: the increasing independence of young people as they grow older, and family unity, particularly with regard to economic welfare. These forces create dilemmas in deciding who should receive benefits:

i) Paying benefits directly to young people interposes a state presence between child and parent. It may grant a young person a degree of independence that parents, in belief of their own values, were not otherwise ready to grant;

ii) Making certain benefits payable only when young people are independent may encourage them to leave home before they and their families are ready;

iii) Paying benefits directly to young people may also hurt family welfare if it is at the expense of support payments to parents;

iv) Paying benefits only to parents may artificially extend young persons' dependency, which may drive them to other activities to get their own resources. It certainly denies to some extent their legitimacy as individuals.

In testing income and setting benefit levels, authorities should take into account whether a young person is living at home or is "independent". In 1982, one in every nine 15-19 year-olds was living alone, married, or in a *de facto* marriage. This is a sizeable number of young people who, because of their independent status, are likely to be under especially strong pressure to earn money to meet their immediate economic needs and, in the process, sacrifice education and training activities and their long-run pay-offs. In determining eligibility and setting benefit levels, authorities should recognise the economic implications of the difference between living with one's family and living independently, and consider the need for lower eligibility thresholds and higher benefit levels for young people living independently. At the same time, however, authorities should be sensitive to the possible impacts of income support arrangements on the behaviour of young people in moving towards independence.

In this regard, authorities should be sensitive to the impact of their actions on young people and their families.

Income support for young people may be the most sensitive area in which the State can intervene, because it can interfere with family patterns of dependency. Australian authorities should be well tuned to popular sentiment – and not just the sentiment of young people. Many young people, those from low-income families especially, contribute to the support of their families directly through money they earn, or indirectly by entitling their parents to payments through the Family Assistance Allowance or Secondary Allowance Scheme. Changes in income support arrangements which reduce family income or direct payments to young people instead of their parents may be unnecessarily disruptive or create undue economic hardship if authorities do not take cognizance of established patterns of dependency.

Conclusions about an Overall Scheme

Not only are the current income support arrangements for youth complex and inconsistent, they serve little apparent purpose beyond income transfer. Income support for old-age pensioners is a social obligation to make the later years of life as pleasant as possible. But it is a terminal proposition. Income support for young people has to lead somewhere. Since young people are just getting their lives underway, the Australian authorities have a responsibility to make sure that income support does more than provide money. It should also provide opportunity. The examiners found too little evidence of income support arrangements complementing other policies in the pursuit of basic national goals.

The current income support arrangements for young people should be overhauled to improve:

i) Short-term socio-economic equality;
ii) Long-term socio-economic equality;
iii) The education and skill level of the labour force;
iv) The ability of low-income young people to make choices without regard to financial considerations.

In order to serve these purposes, the examiners recommend a system meeting three conditions:

- Income tested: eligibility for benefits beyond minimum allowances should depend on need. Need should reflect family income and own income, and relationship to family. Some benefit payments should be made to parents with limited income;
- Favoured choice: the level of benefits should increase according to whether a young person is unemployed, in education, training, or tertiary education;
- Graduated: benefit levels should increase with age; benefits paid to parents should shift to children as they grow older.

Eligibility for income support should begin when young persons reach age 16, and benefit levels should depend first on what is deemed to be minimally adequate.

The examiners recognise the income support scheme they are proposing as an enabling scheme for young people. It provides choice but does not maximise unlimited choice. It is unlikely that any OECD country can afford to subsidise a scheme that permits young people to do whatever they want; the social and economic costs are too high. The scheme does favour choices that, in the view of the examiners, are likely to be good for Australia. Certainly Australian authorities will have their own menu of preference. But the examiners strongly urge them to retain the principle of using their income support schemes for young people to support a larger social and economic agenda.

NOTES AND REFERENCES

1. "Poverty statistics" in Australia are not really adequate for evaluating economic hardship because the poverty lines are not derived on the basis of absolute need. Instead, they use a definition of poverty that is, for all practical purposes, referenced to income distribution.

2. Sources for data on income decile share of income

Year	Source
1968-69	Australian Bureau of Statistics (ABS), *Social Indicators, No. 2 – 1978*. p. 105. Catalogue No. 4101.0,
1973-74	ABS *Social Indicators No. 3 – 1980*, p. 158. Catalogue No. 4104.0,
1978-79	ABS *Income Distribution, Australia*, 1978-79: Supplement to Social Indicators No. 3, p. 2. Catalogue No. 4108.0,
1981-82	ABS *Income and Housing Survey : Income of Individuals, Australia, 1981-82*, p. 6. Catalogue No. 6502.6.

3. OECD, *Public Expenditures on Income Maintenance Programmes*, (Paris: 1976), pp. 108-109.
4. Australian Bureau of Statistics (ABS), *The Labour Force: Australia; 1984*, Catalogue No. 62030, p. 19.
5. ABS, *Weekly Earnings of Employees (Distribution) Australia, August 1983* Catalogue No. 6310.0, p. 11.
6. ABS, *Estimated Resident Population by Sex and Age: States and Territories of Australia, June 1971 to June 1981*, Catalogue No. 3201.0, pp. 36, 46.
7. OECD, *Revenue Statistics on OECD Member Countries: 1965-1983*, (OECD, Paris: 1984), p. 84.
8. See also Bureau of Labour Market Research, *Employment and Training Programmes for Young People: Analysis of Assistance in 1980-81* (Australian Government Publishing Service, Canberra: 1983).
9. See Commission of the European Communities, *Comparative Tables of the Social Security Schemes of the Member States of the European Communities: 12th Edition* (Office for Official Publications of the European Communities, Luxembourg: 1982)

    See also U.S. Department of Health and Human Services, *Social Security Programs throughout the World: 1981* (U.S. Government Printing Office, Washington, D.C.: 1982).
10. University of Melbourne, Institute of Applied Economic and Social Research; *Poverty Lines: Australia, August 1983*, (December 1983.)

    See also Office of Youth Affairs and the Social Welfare Policy Secretariat, *Income Support for Young People* (Australian Government Publishing Service, Canberra: 1984).

Chapter 5

AN ENTITLEMENT FOR YOUNG PEOPLE

Taken *in toto,* the policies and arrangements in Australia for employment, income support, and especially education and training, lack a sense of overriding purpose when it comes to serving young people. Activities are carried out too much in isolation in each area, with too little attention given to what the activities are trying to accomplish individually and collectively, with respect to preparing young people for employment, and preparing them more generally for adulthood.

Because activities in all three areas play crucial roles in the development of young people, the various institutions involved require at a minimum that they be geared explicitly to serving a purpose beyond their own narrowly defined institutional mission:

  i) Education must be geared not simply to achieving a certain retention rate, but better to equip young people for making decisions about work and future training;

 ii) Training must be geared not just for raising competence levels, but for improving the job-readiness and employability of young people; and their adaptability to changing conditions;

iii) Income support must not simply be income transfer for meeting immediate economic needs, but it must be an "enabling device" that allows young people to pursue education and training or whatever activities are considered to be in the public good;

 iv) Income support also must be arranged so that young people from poor families can afford, in the short term, to stay enrolled in education and training activities.

It can be argued that the various institutional arrangements for education and training, as they exist now, can be made to work together. But, the various components comprising the different arrangements are not administered to be compatible, or even designed to serve purposes that are compatible. The existing income support arrangements are poor enabling mechanisms and, in some cases, discourage desirable education and training activities. Moreover, except in the cases of young people going through secondary education and on to higher education – the standard track – it is up to young people themselves to take the initiatives in identifying and choosing options, and arranging the sequence of activities. Those who thrive in the system do not succeed because of the good design of the system. Rather, their success reflects their own initiative, the influence of friends, families and peers, and chance.

Finally, the current arrangements certainly do nothing to redress socio-economic equality. In a process that lacks formal articulation between institutions and relies so heavily on the initiative of young people, the most disadvantaged ones are those more likely to fall through the cracks, leaving school or training without adequate preparation for work and adulthood. They are less likely to receive information from informal networks about the various opportunities, or to receive encouragement to pursue education or training opportunities. They are the ones under the greatest pressure to earn money immediately to contribute to support their families or to become economically independent.

At a minimum, the various services, programmes and activities embodied in the education, training, employment and income support arrangements for young people need to be changed along the lines suggested in the preceding chapters. But that is not enough for youth policies to be effective. Those individual elements need to be orchestrated so that the transition by a young person from one element to another is not a random proposition, and so that young people are not entirely on their own in trying to assure that they are prepared for adulthood and employment. A broader form of accountability is needed to accomplish this, one that cuts across institutional lines.

The Need for Structure

What is needed in Australia is a commitment shared among the various institutional providers to do their defined job and to prepare young people for the transition to the next step in their development. This does not require a high degree of centralised leadership because it is really young people themselves who should make decisions about how they want to proceed. But it does require a structure to assure that young people have the information they need to make informed decisions, and to facilitate the transition from one institutional base to another required to execute those decisions. An "Entitlement" is one approach to give form and structure to such a commitment.

The examiners' views on an Entitlement are discussed below. The discussion outlines the concept of such an Entitlement and its purpose, and then briefly suggests the relevant institutional arrangements.

The examiners recommend that the Australian authorities establish an Entitlement, with the purpose of guaranteeing to all young people in Australia that when they leave the overall education and training system, they are adequately equipped for adulthood and the world of work. The Entitlement should do this by assuring that every young person will have the opportunity, before entering the labour market, to pursue secondary education through year twelve, further education or training (as an alternative to upper secondary education) or apprenticeship training. For those not choosing any of those alternatives, the Entitlement should guarantee at least a basic preparation for adulthood, living independently, and the world of work.

Operation of an Entitlement should be delivered through two complementary sets of institutional arrangements: A "Youth Entitlement" for those young people continuing through upper secondary education, TAFE, or apprenticeship, and an "Entitlement Year" for those who do not complete a programme of post-compulsory study.

The Purpose

The purpose of the Youth Entitlement should be to make sure that those young people choosing to pursue post-compulsory education and training can carry out their plans more easily, and when they finish, will be equipped for work and adulthood. The Youth Entitlement should assure first that there is adequate articulation between compulsory secondary education and the various post-compulsory activities, to assure *i)* that students have adequate information about their options, and *ii)* they have appropriate assistance in making the transition between institutions.

Once young people are engaged in post-compulsory education and training, the Youth Entitlement should ensure that they receive information and counselling about further education and training opportunities, work preparation, basic training and life skills training. In this way they will be better equipped to take the initial choice about their careers and to follow up this choice by appropriate training for career planning.

The purpose of the Entitlement Year should be to act as a "safety net" to "catch" those young people who are not continuing secondary education, not enrolling in TAFE or apprenticeship, and making sure they have the opportunity to receive at least a minimum level of preparation for employment and adulthood. When they complete the Entitlement Year, these young people should:

- *i)* Be equipped to make informed decisions about career plans, and know what action is necessary to fulfil those plans;
- *ii)* Receive the preparation they need to have a better chance of finding employment, or if they change their minds, of either continuing secondary education, entering apprenticeship or institution-based training; and
- *iii)* Have a credential to reflect what has been learned.

The Entitlement Year for those not continuing in mainstream options should provide for a range of "graduated" activities to allow for different stages of readiness among young persons participating, and to permit progressive development:

- *i)* Occupational and labour market information to help young people make decisions about what occupations or general occupational areas they would like to enter;
- *ii)* Orientation to the world of work, and coaching in life skills to prepare young persons for adulthood;
- *iii)* Job search assistance and at least some subsidised part-time jobs for youths participating in the Entitlement Year and interested in working;
- *iv)* Pre-apprenticeship and other pre-vocational training for those interested in entering apprenticeship but unable to arrange an apprentice position;
- *v)* Counselling to help young people decide what courses of education and skill development they should follow; and
- *vi)* A credential indicating knowledge of the world of work and job readiness skills for those going on to employment, and assistance in finding employment.

The Entitlement Year activities generally should be targeted for young people when they leave secondary education and are intending to enter the labour force. However, recognising that some young people may not be interested in preparing for permanent employment right away, young people, by right, should be eligible to participate in Entitlement Year activities through age 24.

Administrative and Institutional Arrangements

Institutional arrangements for the Youth Entitlement should be based on: *i)* improvements in the content of education and training activities as delineated in Chapter 3, and *ii)* improved articulation among the various education and training institutions. Arrangements for the Entitlement Year activities will depend on the adequacy and availability of a range of local programmes. The five activities recommended for the Entitlement Year are similar to those carried out under the Community Youth Support Scheme (CYSS), the Education Programme for Unemployed Youth (EPUY), the Special Youth Employment and

Training Programme (SYETP), and the pre-apprentice/pre-vocational schemes. Under an Entitlement Year scheme, the choice of institutional provider would probably depend on assessments by local authorities as to who is best equipped to provide the needed services[1]. The principal objective in changing the arrangements would be to assure better a connection between other "mainstream" education and training activities and to establish an alternative, non-education-based credential.

The Youth Entitlement and the Entitlement Year should be administered locally. In the case of the former, this should include assuring that all young people are informed about the availability of Entitlement Year activities, and overseeing the establishment of the appropriate linkages between secondary education and TAFE and apprenticeship. In the case of the Entitlement Year, administrative responsibility should include notifying young people of their eligibility for the Entitlement Year (and keeping track of those who do not enroll right away and reminding them of their options), and arranging services.

The Youth Entitlement and the Entitlement Year could be administered by local offices of the Commonwealth Employment Service as the Danish Entitlement pilot project was managed. It could also be managed by local authorities, in co-operation with secondary education, TAFE, and tertiary education officials, as the Swedish Planning Councils do[2]. It might be watched over by a local committee, on the British model, representing employers, unions, educators, local authorities and voluntary organisations.

In proposing an Entitlement, the examiners want to distinguish carefully between what they propose and the various forms of youth guarantee and allowance proposals that they encountered during the review. The examiners see a Youth Entitlement and the Entitlement Year primarily as a set of services and institutional arrangements that are geared to providing information and basic training facilitating choice among subsequent education, training, and employment options. Taken together, the Youth Entitlement and the Entitlement Year should create a safety net that assures that all young people, when they leave secondary school, TAFE or apprenticeship, have at least the basic information they need to make informed, clear choices, and have the preparation to take the next step in their own development.

Indeed, the examiners found the focus of debate in Australia on the topic to be narrow, and their suggestions are therefore intended to help broaden the debate in Australia.

Redirecting the Debate for Australia

The examiners find their objectives and priorities with respect to a Youth Entitlement to be quite different from those dominating the debate in Australia. Though the Australian authorities suggested, in the terms of reference for the review, that a youth guarantee or allowance proposal might be based on "a comprehensive and integrated approach to support services for young people"[3], the topic was treated much more narrowly in discussions with government authorities and advocates speaking on behalf of young people. The discussions and debate on the topic in Australia have been preoccupied with what are real and vexing problems in the income support arrangements for young people, while ignoring far more fundamental and important questions of gaps in services, institutional access, and ultimately, the state of unpreparedness with which so many young people leave school and enter the labour market.

The examiners conclude that the present form of debate on youth guarantees and allowances is the product of four factors:

i) An absence of leadership (probably at the state level) that could create a unified set of objectives with regard to what happens to young people, which would better guide policies in secondary schools and TAFE institutions;

ii) The fact that the income support responsibilities rest squarely with the Commonwealth government;

iii) The fact that under the existing income support provisions, unemployment benefits are the most readily available and most generous of all sources of income support, and require the least in return;

iv) The fact that the immediate effect of various income support measures (complete with their inconsistencies and distorted incentives) is readily apparent to the young people (far more apparent than changes in institutional arrangements, for example).

The first factor makes the goal of "a comprehensive and integrated approach to support services for young people" a difficult one to pursue for two reasons. First, it defines change in institutional terms, suggesting different roles and different relationships. This impinges on established practices and resource allocation patterns, and introduces a new set of vested interests (those of the institutions) to the discussion that may not always be consistent with the interests of young people. Second, determining what changes are needed requires assessing institutional governance arrangements that are primarily under state and local control, and that vary from state to state. The interventions needed to close the gaps in institutional arrangements cannot be carried out only at a national level.

In contrast, the other three factors reinforce the focus of debate on income support issues. First, the changes are primarily aimed at policy, not institutions. Second, the authority for change is vested at a single level of government. Third, the change objectives are easily identified and the results are easily observed (and evaluated).

The examiners find the focus of the Australian debate on youth guarantees and allowances to be fundamentally misdirected because it subordinates questions of education, training, and employment policy to questions of income support policy. The shortcomings in education, training, and employment arrangements (discussed in Chapters 2 and 3) have far greater long-term implications for the general health of the Australian economy and for socio-economic equality, than shortcomings in the income support arrangements (discussed in Chapter 4). As a matter of public priority, it seems far more important that there be adequate arrangements for education, training, and employment and that access to those arrangements be equitable, than whether income support arrangements are appropriately "tuned". The principal purpose of a Youth Entitlement should be to make sure all young people are given at least an adequate preparation for work and adulthood. The examiners view the principal purpose of a youth allowance, though important, to be short-term and, perhaps, temporary, and appropriately central to a larger debate on income support policies in general, not youth entitlements.

Experience in Other Countries

In their experience with youth guarantee and entitlement programmes, other countries have emphasized guaranteed opportunities for education and training first. Some have tried limited employment guarantees. None has posed income support as the pre-eminent goal or centerpiece of any "guarantee". Four OECD countries have recent experience with youth guarantee and entitlement programmes. From 1980 to 1983, Denmark conducted an experimental youth guarantee programme in two counties for school-leavers and unemployed youth up to the age of 24. Sweden recently launched a nationwide programme guaranteeing education and training and at least a part-time job to all unemployed 18 and 19 year-olds. The United Kingdom has conducted its major youth training and employment interventions as a guarantee of sorts for school-leavers who are unable to find work. The scheme was overhauled in 1983, to strengthen the training component and include those entering employment as well as those out of work. From 1978 to 1982, the United States conducted an entitlement programme in 17 cities and counties to guarantee employment for 16-19 year-olds from low-income families if they remained enrolled in or (for early-leavers) if they returned to education or training.

All of these schemes have shared two elements: they have placed a heavy emphasis on the role of education and training, work experience, and they have rejected "passive" financial assistance. In the Danish, British and American schemes, these education and training opportunities have been seen as essential for improving the employability of young people. Though the Swedish programme does not require unemployed persons to enroll in training or education in order to be eligible for a job, the programme treats education and training as a substitute for work. The Danish and American schemes, with their heavier emphasis on education and training, feature more structured roles for the involvement of those institutions. In Denmark, the Ministry of Education was a partner with the Ministry of Labour in launching and overseeing the guarantee programme. At the local level, education and training institutions were involved in counselling and guidance activities in expanding education and training opportunities. In the American scheme, local schools were involved in providing counselling and guidance, and also in maintaining contact with employers. The overhauled British scheme has effectively created a new kind of vocational preparation for young persons in private companies.

The various entitlement and guarantee schemes have been based on a deliberate policy preference for "active" over "passive" income assistance. In Denmark, Sweden and the United Kingdom where school-leavers and other unemployed youths can establish eligibility for unemployment benefits relatively easily, authorities adopted the schemes as alternatives to "passive" income support that would simply provide financial aid. Though not everyone in the schemes in Denmark and Sweden was receiving unemployment benefits, participation was treated as a requirement for eligibility for unemployment benefits. In the United States, where the entitlement scheme's target population was unlikely to be eligible for unemployment insurance, "passive" income assistance was less an issue.

In general, income support provisions have been subordinate considerations in the guarantee and entitlement schemes in other countries. At most, income needs of youths are recognised as being important in determining whether or not young people can continue in education or training. Then, as in the American and Swedish programmes, work has been made available as a source of income. In this context, income support was seen as an enabling strategy to permit young people to participate. Nowhere have youth guarantee and entitlement programmes started as income transfer schemes and then been developed backwards as rationales or conditions for receiving income transfer.

A Strategy for Launching a Youth Entitlement and Entitlement Year

The entitlement scheme suggested by the examiners depends heavily on improving arrangements for education, training, employment and income support, and improving the relationship of those arrangements to one another. The entitlement is one way of putting those arrangements together so that those young persons most likely to be at risk in the labour market are assured of at least a foundation of preparation.

For the Youth Entitlement and the Entitlement Year to have meaning, the kinds of improvements suggested in the preceding chapters need to be adopted. But it is also important that the current debate in Australia on a Youth Entitlement move in a fundamentally different direction, away from its preoccupation with income support.

The examiners strongly urge that the Commonwealth government exert a leadership role in redefining the public debate on an entitlement for young people in Australia.

A first step in redirecting the public debate might be to separate income support from the issue of an entitlement. This certainly is justifiable from a logical point of view because a Youth Entitlement (at least as envisioned here) would be targeted on a broader population than income support provisions. Further, income support should be treated separately because it is also a purely Commonwealth function. While this may polarise the debate over rationalising income support measures more than it already is by turning it into a single issue, it is necessary if the important, but less obvious, institutional issues are to be treated appropriately.

The second step the Commonwealth could take to redefine the debate is to put the Youth Entitlement on the agenda of State Ministers of Youth Affairs, Education and Employment. Although there is certainly a leadership role and possibly a management or "traffic director" role for Commonwealth authorities developing and operating a Youth Entitlement, the heart of an entitlement is the services provided under authority of the state. State authorities need to be involved, and the sooner the better. In any event, state and local authorities will need to be convinced of the need for improvements in education/training and employment arrangements. Whether all states decide to pursue development of an entitlement programme is not as important as steering state-level discussions in that direction.

The Commonwealth should set a deadline for January 1986 for establishing the Entitlement Year and the Youth Entitlement.

Whatever date is established for starting an Entitlement will be arbitrary and somewhat meaningless; a truly workable set of entitlement arrangements cannot start until all the elements are in place, including those under the control of three disparate, and in certain respects, autonomous levels of government. However, by January 1986, the Commonwealth should be able to complete the needed changes in income support arrangements. Regardless of who eventually administers the entitlement arrangements locally, the Commonwealth Employment Service should take the initiative to begin developing the management capacity locally. At a minimum, at the time, the CES also should be able to make available to eligible young people occupational outlook and career planning information oriented to local labour markets, and job search and placement assistance on a more systematic basis than is provided now.

The Commonwealth should facilitate and monitor implementation of the Entitlement Year and the Youth Entitlement

During implementation of the two, it will be essential for the Commonwealth to play an important "hub" role in *i)* tracking how individual states manage the entitlement arrangements; *ii)* providing assistance in the development of the needed infrastructures; and *iii)* establishing communication and consultation channels among state and local authorities responsible for the entitlement arrangements, to speed up the dissemination and exchange of effective practices.

In monitoring implementation, the Commonwealth should report on the progress in institutional arrangements initially, but stress assessment of impacts on individuals over the longer run. Such assessment of individual impact should report on the distribution of young people across the different options (education, training, employment, Entitlement activities, unemployed), and should follow up those who go through the Entitlement Year to see what their experience is with respect to employment, education and training.

Conclusion

The examiners think it important that the Australian authorities adopt some form of a Youth Entitlement and Entitlement Year. There are simply too many young people who leave the formal education and training institutions in Australia unprepared to work or make informed decisions about further education or training. The Entitlement is needed to make sure that all young people receive the information they need to decide about what occupations they would like to enter and to help them carry out plans for career preparation, regardless of whether they continue secondary education, enter TAFE, an apprenticeship or employment.

NOTES AND REFERENCES

1. It is important that whoever is responsible for these activities be closely linked with secondary education and TAFE at least. This has not always been the case with the Commonwealth youth programmes such as CYSS, EPUY and SYETP. For that reason, the examiners are not suggesting that those programmes be adapted to the Entitlement Year. In areas where there is a record of co-operation between those programmes and local education and training institutions, those programmes might be retained. Otherwise, their activities might be transplanted to another institutional base. For a more detailed discussion of a Youth Entitlement based on adapting the Commonwealth youth programmes, see W. Merrilees, "Towards an Integrated System of Vocational Training Programmes: The Youth Guarantee Concept", in the *Journal of Industrial Relations,* (December 1983), pp. 478-482.
2. See "Preliminary Note on Experiments with a Youth Guarantee Scheme", Danish Ministry of Labour and Ministry of Education: 1980; and Helen Ginsburg, "How Sweden Combats Youth Unemployment Among Young and Older Workers", in *Monthly Labor Review,* (United States Department of Labor, October 1982).
3. Such as that suggested in W. Merrilees, "Towards an Integrated System of Vocational Training Programmes: The Youth Guarantee Concept", in the *Journal of Industrial Relations,* (December 1983), pp. 465-485.

Chapter 6

RATIONALISING AND DECENTRALISING GOVERNANCE ARRANGEMENTS

One of the harsh realities confronting policy-makers trying to improve youth policies in Australia is the fact that remedies depend on the participation of largely autonomous players. The Commonwealth government has assumed a leadership role in the youth policy development process, but whatever policies come out of that process will necessarily require the involvement of state and local governments, communities, unions, employers and young people themselves, if the policies are to work. They must be based not only on a "conceptual" consensus about what the problems are and what kinds of intervention are needed to solve them, but on a consensus on governance and power as well. There must be agreement on who develops measures, who implements them and who manages them. The examiners found little consensus on such issues. This concerns them because without clear agreement about roles and responsibilities, and without participation by all the players needed for schemes to work, youth policies will be only partial solutions at best.

There are two deficiencies in the process of consensus-building that threaten the workability of remedies:

  i) The role of the various parties taking part in formulating, implementing and managing remedies is not well balanced; and
  ii) Accountability is not sufficiently defined or enforced.

These deficiencies and ways to correct them are discussed below. Though the discussion focuses on the deficiencies in governance and power-sharing arrangements, it is not meant to imply that the Commonwealth attempts to fashion new youth policies for Australia are wrong, and it certainly does not suggest that the Commonwealth should not assume the leadership role in the process. Youth unemployment is a national problem in Australia with national consequences, and requires national solutions. It is therefore essential that the highest level of government provide the guiding force in the effort to solve the problem.

But the examiners find it essential that the Commonwealth take special care that the leadership role does not turn into an overall management role. Instead, in its leadership role, the Commonwealth should serve as a catalyst, to produce changes at other levels of government, in what they do with regard to their education and training responsibilities, for example. Commonwealth resources might be used in the process of facilitating that change. But it is essential that the Commonwealth does not superimpose policies that overlap existing selected local policies unless there is a clear consensus favouring such an approach.

Balancing and Rationalising Roles[1]

In the course of their visit and in reviewing background material, the examiners were favourably impressed by Commonwealth efforts to conduct an open enquiry into the causes of youth unemployment and possible solutions. The Commonwealth encouraged consultative activities such as those carried on by the Youth Affairs Council of Australia and through meetings convened by the Commonwealth and State Youth Affairs Ministers. Indeed, the work and the meetings of the OECD examiners were part of that process of enquiry, presenting forums for hearing the views of young people, employers and unions as well as those of various levels of government engaged in providing services for young people.

But the examiners also noted that the consultative processes were by and large one-way: feeding views to the Commonwealth. They found too little evidence of the Commonwealth using its consultative processes as a vehicle for developing consensus. Perhaps the examiners' visit was too early in the current problem review and policy formulation process for the Commonwealth to begin "reversing the flow of consultation" soliciting reactions to federal proposals. But in any event the examiners observed that the various players expected a "consultative process" that would yield a final policy package being handed down from Canberra as a *fait accompli,* with little room for negotiation. Prior programmes and policies in the youth employment area were cited as precedents and the basis for the pessimistic views that the examiners found.

This highly-centralised approach, to the extent it exists, interferes with consensus-building in two ways. First, it limits the kind of detailed information needed to assure that general policies can be adapted to particular local needs and circumstances. Second, it places the contributions of consulted parties so far from the final policy outcomes that it is hard for them to see their contribution or have much sense of ownership over what is finally produced.

The examiners found limitations in the consultative processes especially disturbing because they may interfere with rationalisation of responsibilities of government. Rationalisation of functions is of course essential at the Commonwealth level, as those involved in the youth policy review process have agreed. Policies conducted by different departments need to be consistent and compatible with one another. Indeed, much of the discussion in the preceding chapters might help guide that rationalisation of functions.

But there also needs to be rationalisation of the roles played by different levels of government and the social partners in implementing and managing youth policies, because Commonwealth policies cover only a part of the spectrum of services that should be directed at young people. This requires rationalisation *between* levels of government to assure that policies are compatible and consistent, and, when taken together, are comprehensive. This process of rationalisation between levels of government is likely to be a more ambiguous process in which negotiation and mutual consent replace administrative *fiat* as the means for accomplishing it.

This second process of rationalisation should be guided by the same criteria that other OECD countries have followed in decentralising the provision of many social services; i) *keep routine decision-making regarding services as close to the client as possible; and* ii) *retain certain strategic resource allocation, technical assistance, goal-setting and evaluation functions at the national level.*

More specifically, in rationalising Commonwealth activities, national authorities should distinguish between two kinds of functions and treat them separately:

  i) Those functions that are clearly state and local responsibilities; and
  ii) Those functions that are presently Commonwealth responsibilities.

The Commonwealth strategy should then be to provide the support to help state and local authorities in carrying out their responsibilities, and better rationalise those activities that are purely Commonwealth responsibilities. These separate functions are discussed below.

Facilitating State and Local Functions

Three essential parts of any comprehensive set of youth policies – secondary education, TAFE, and apprenticeship training – are not under federal authority. The Commonwealth has no standing to assume "control" in managing how these functions relate to one another, in enforcing a set of choices for young people, or in requiring certain "improvements" in who is served and how they are served. Instead, the Commonwealth should provide five strategic support functions – continuing what it already does and expanding into new areas. Five activities seem especially important:

i) *Developing, testing and documenting the effectiveness of education, training and related counselling and guidance activities for increasing female enrolment in "non-traditional" courses of study and training;*

ii) *Continuing to support innovations in secondary curriculum and pedagogic approaches, including the use of computer-based and other micro-electronic technology as instructional tools and courses of study; documenting the effectiveness of such innovations and disseminating results;*

iii) *Developing alternative standards and measures for evaluating educational and vocational skill competences;*

iv) *Identifying practitioners at the state and local levels, in unions and among employers who have first-hand knowledge of managing innovative and effective activities;*

v) *Encouraging the development of the necessary state and local infrastructures for managing certain functions that might be delegated from higher to lower levels of government.*

The principle guiding these activities should be to provide those in state and local government and employers and unions with the models they need for improving the overall effectiveness of education and training activities. Administrative coercion should not be exercised in carrying out these activities, because it runs the risk of putting the Commonwealth in the position of prescribing means for reaching certain policy goals. However, the Commonwealth should establish certain policy goals and use the power it has with regard to allocation of resources to provide incentives for achieving those goals. Such goals might include target enrolment levels for women in apprenticeship and target retention levels for secondary schools. However, the competent officials should be free to decide for themselves how to achieve overall goals by adopting programmes and policies that are best suited to their circumstances.

Federal Functions

Among the various governmental functions that concern young people, only two are squarely under Commonwealth control: income support and labour market programmes.

In rationalising the relationship of these functions to other functions concerning young people, the Commonwealth should delegate management authority to as low a level of government as practical. The principle for delegating authority should be for the Commonwealth to set clear outcome objectives and eligibility guidelines, for example, and delegate authority for deciding how those objectives are best accomplished and guidelines met. The point of delegating responsibility should be to enhance the ability of those serving young people to adapt services and modes of delivering those services to local circumstances and the particular needs of young people.

Under the Community Employment Programme and the Participation and Equity Programme, the Commonwealth is already increasing state and local discretion (although, some argue, not enough) in deciding what kinds of activities to fund, and who should participate in the programmes. This should continue, and the Commonwealth should consider expanding state and local management control, also with regard to income support measures, such as the Youth Entitlement.

The Commonwealth should encourage, document, evaluate, and possibly provide financial support to state-level attempts to delegate authority and decentralise services. In particular, the Commonwealth should examine attempts at decentralisation such as those in South Australia and Victoria. In South Australia, the state Ministry of Education is exploring ways of delegating to the local level authority the power to make decisions on how to reallocate secondary school resources in the face of declining school enrolments[2]. In Victoria there is interest at the state and local level in reviewing the full range of youth services, and in seeing where development and management of services could be further decentralised to local authorities[3].

In considering to whom to delegate authority, the Commonwealth needs to take account of not just the content of programmes, but the nature of organisations managing them as well.

For example, traditional secondary schools may not always be the best vehicles for educational innovation under the Participation and Equity Programme if there are large numbers of early school-leavers permanently "turned off" by them. Local CES offices similarly may not be able to attract females trying to enter non-traditional occupations if CES is seen as contributing to patterns of occupational segregation by sex.

The Commonwealth should make sure that community interests, such as those reflected in certain Community Youth Support Scheme (CYSS) projects and women's support groups are represented. In supporting CYSS and special employment initiatives such as the Hunter Equal Opportunity Programme over the last several years, the Commonwealth has helped create a network of community-based organisations that frequently provide the infrastructure that succeeds in reaching many young people not served well by more traditional arrangements. While the examiners recognise that community organisations are not uniformly effective, many are. Where they are well managed and have the confidence and involvement of young people and the community at large, they should be considered as candidates for managing certain decentralised activities.

Accountability in a Decentralised System

Services for youth in Australia need to be evaluated first and foremost on the basis of what happens to young people. For this to happen Australian authorities need to evaluate policy interventions to determine whether persons secure jobs in occupations related to their training, what their earnings are, whether high-risk youth who stay longer in secondary school go into different training or career paths than in the past, whether girls following "non-traditional" paths for career preparation indeed get into non-traditional jobs.

Some of this can be accomplished by collecting more complete administrative data. For example, TAFE institutions and apprenticeship programmes need to provide more detailed breakdowns by sex of precisely the kind of training provided. In doing this, top level administrators must be careful not to impose excessive reporting requirements. But a balance needs to be struck in favour of more detailed data on programme substance and persons served than is available now. Perhaps as part of a trade-off there are other data requirements that could be reduced. (It would be useful to determine whether data that already exist could be used better.) There are no easy guides to how this is handled. The view of the examiners, though, is that the present arrangements fail to provide certain basic information needed to make informed management decisions.

But besides getting better management information, the examiners believe that Australian authorities need more complete information on the kind of preparation individuals receive and their subsequent employment and earning histories. This kind of information, because it must be collected over time, is expensive and difficult to collect, especially where the youth population is a highly mobile one. But labour market and education authorities in the United States, Canada and France have demonstrated that usable information can be collected economically on a sample basis. Indeed, the Australian Department of Employment and Industrial Relations has plans for launching a longitudinal panel, though details on the kind of data to be collected were not available at the time of the examiners' visit. The examiners urge that the longitudinal survey sample enough young people and include sufficiently detailed information on training and education to provide some insights about the effectiveness of those activities and the impact of policy changes.

Conclusions

The solutions to Australia's youth unemployment problem require an amalgamation of services that, in a constitutional sense, are ungovernable, because responsibilities are spread across three levels of government, unions, employers and communities. But the solutions are manageable through a process of negotiation and mutual consent. To make this happen the examiners believe the Commonwealth needs to exercise a leadership role in:

i) Facilitating a process (which it has already started) of reaching consensus among relevant parties on youth policies and setting specific objectives that everyone can support;

ii) Rationalising functional responsibilities among the different parties to assure that they are consistent, compatible, and as comprehensive as possible, and decentralising provision of services; and

iii) Improving accountability in the policies serving young people.

But the Commonwealth will be careful about exercising its leadership role in this process with a very light touch. The joint action needed can only come by consensus, not coercion[4].

NOTES AND REFERENCES

1. The examiners do not equate decentralisation of authority over particular services with decentralisation of responsibility for financing such services. In fact, they found the Australian system of finance to be commendable. It relies heavily on revenues collected by the Commonwealth through a progressive income tax system with much of the revenues passed back to the states, for education, for example. Where the examiners recommend that programmatic authority for what are now Commonwealth programmes be passed to lower levels of government, they envision that the Commonwealth would continue to finance such programmes.
2. M.P. Hewton, "Towards the Transfer of Education Buildings to the Local Community – The Elizabeth Experience", prepared for the OECD Conference on Provision and Management of School Buildings (Adelaide, May 1983).
3. See "The Role of Local Government in the Planning, Co-ordination and Provision of Youth Services in Victoria", prepared by the Municipal Association of Victoria, November 1983; and "A Strategy for the Co-ordination and Development of Youth Policy in Victoria: A Discussion Paper", prepared by the Department of the Premier and Cabinet, (November 1983).
4. See OECD, *Manpower Policy in Australia,* (Paris, 1975), p. 112.

Chapter 7

A FRAMEWORK FOR NEW INITIATIVES

There is an immediate problem in Australia of unemployment and under-employment among young people. But there is a long-term problem as well: low levels of educational attainment and occupational skills, and unequal access to the education and training opportunities that do exist.

This report has dealt with both problems. But, for three reasons, the second problem is of greater concern to the examiners. First, if left unattended, it will contribute to structural unemployment and socio-economic inequality, and the Australian labour force will lack the skill and education requirements the economy needs to compete in world markets. Second, correcting it requires long-term changes in education, training and income support arrangements. Third, it needs to be highlighted or it will be overshadowed by the youth unemployment and underemployment problem which is producing very visible and immediate economic hardship.

The discussion below presents a framework for new youth policies based on the conclusions and recommendations presented in the preceding chapters. It establishes priorities among those recommendations and suggests how education, training, employment and income support policies might be better connected.

Improving Preparation for Adulthood and Employment

The highest priority for the Australian youth agenda should be to raise educational attainment, increase broad-based occupational skills, and assure that education and training opportunities are accessible without regard to sex or socio-economic status.

There are six deficiencies under the current arrangements:
  i) Girls are underserved and channelled into education and training paths to lower-paying, lower-status jobs;
  ii) Secondary school retention is too low;
  iii) The quality of TAFE training is not clearly documented, its relevance is not assured, and its capacity for expansion is uncertain;
  iv) Apprenticeship training is in danger of becoming obsolete and is too vulnerable to short-term fluctuations in economic activity;
  v) Enterprise-based training is too much of an unknown and uncontrollable factor;
  vi) Access to higher education is biased against girls and disadvantaged young people.

The examiners recommend a six-part strategy for raising education and occupational skill levels.

i) *Equalise opportunities for women*

Secondary, higher and technical further education authorities should increase female enrolments in math, science, technology, and business courses of study. This should be accomplished by strengthening (and initiating where they are absent) counselling, guidance, and positive discrimination programmes.

Apprenticeship authorities should increase female enrolments to the same level as for males. This may require counselling, guidance, and positive discrimination to encourage females to enter occupations traditionally dominated by males, and establishing apprenticeship positions in emerging occupations in areas where females are presently well represented.

ii) *Improve secondary education*

Secondary education authorities should improve the value and attractiveness of secondary education so as to increase retention through year twelve and better equip those who do leave early to make and carry out informed decisions regarding career choices and personal development. This is likely to require updating course offerings, content, instructional techniques, including expanded use of computer-based instruction and more general instruction on the use and application of computer-based technology for *all* students throughout *all* levels of secondary education. There is a need for more educational and vocational counselling including the use of occupational outlook and career planning information well before year ten so that young people can more fully understand their options and the consequences of different choices. There is also a need to allow flexible class scheduling permitting combinations of work and education, and to consider combining production activities and education and training.

Upper secondary education should do more than simply prepare young people for higher education. It should be geared to young people going on to technical training, apprenticeship, and immediate employment as well. This will require a broader curriculum and a more flexible approach to assessment and credentialing of secondary education, an approach that is not dictated by the assessment and entry requirements of higher education.

Young people should be given genuine decision-making authority in the process of improving education and managing new approaches to education, to assure that such changes respond to their needs and preferences.

iii) *Strengthen and expand vocational training opportunities in TAFE*

If the technical and further education institutions are to be effective in providing skill training, they have to assure better that their training is appropriate for labour market needs and they have to know better what they are accomplishing right now with their current resources. The first requires more systematic impact by unions and employers in determining vocational training course offerings, the content of such courses, and how competences are evaluated. The second requires management information to provide details on the exact kind of training persons receive. It also requires evaluative information on what happens to trainees when they go to work and whether they find employment related to their training; how well suited their skills are to the requirements of the job, and what their earnings and employment experiences are. Finally, it requires the development of standards for evaluating skill competences in a way that is useful to trainees, training administrators, unions and employers.

iv) *Modify the management and finance of apprenticeship to improve its viability during economic downturns, and expand apprenticeship into emerging occupational areas*

If apprenticeship is to survive and be available in relatively small enterprises, its costs need to be treated more as fixed costs. This might be accomplished best by requiring employers to retain a fixed proportion of their labour force as apprentices or to pay a levy, which would be refunded to employers providing apprenticeship training. Apprenticeship should be made more feasible financially to small firms through the expansion of group apprenticeship schemes.

Apprenticeship should be expanded into emerging occupational areas. This is likely to require identifying emerging occupational areas where new apprenticeship training could be developed or current arrangements adapted, and determining what competences are required and what training is needed.

v) *Take advantage of enterprise-based training*

Australian authorities need to support and systematise one of Australia's greatest training resources, training provided on the job. There should be support in the form of training subsidies provided to employers under training contracts where they are teaching young people general, transferable skills and competences. Authorities should encourage development (in TAFE, for example) of standards for evaluating competences and to be used as a basis for competence credentials to facilitate the assessment and transferability of competences learned on the job.

vi) *Adapt income support schemes for young people to better assure that they will undertake activities that will increase their economic independence*

Income support benefits should be paid to reward best those activities that benefit young people and society most: education and training. The purpose of this strategy should be to assure that young people do not have to forego education and training activities that will produce long-term benefits in order to maximise the short-term income received in the form of unemployment benefits.

Income support benefits should be income-tested. Targeting benefits will make it more affordable for Australia to meet all the needs of the most disadvantaged youth thus enabling them to participate in education and training. Targeting also will minimise the chance of income support subsidising choices that better-off young people would have made anyway.

Eligibility for unemployment benefits should be restricted. Unemployment benefits should help support job search activities. If, after a period of job search, a young person cannot find work owing to limited education or a lack of vocational skills, continued eligibility should be contingent on enrolment in education or training, or participation in community service schemes.

Improving Employment Prospects for Young People

Improved education and training opportunities will fall far short of solving the unemployment and underemployment problem for young people in Australia. Both general economic measures and selective employment measures are needed to assure that more jobs are available and that work is spread equitably.

A necessary ingredient of any overall strategy for improving employment prospects for young people is to pursue those macro-economic policies that improve overall employment. Young people in Australia cannot be sheltered from the effects of the current recession. However, in the short and medium term, at least, before the effects of concerted changes in education and training policies can be felt, employment growth, if it follows past patterns, will not be particularly favourable to youth. Without extraordinary measures, girls and young women will not be able to overcome firmly entrenched patterns of discrimination, lower wages, and occupational segregation. More generally, employment growth will be weaker in the industry and occupational areas where young people are over-represented, and is likely to be increasingly in part-time and marginal employment. Three kinds of selective measures are needed to assure that young people benefit from improved economic conditions.

i) *Reallocate existing jobs to favour young people more*

In certain areas, the Australian authorities can increase youth employment by redirecting job placement resources and those hiring policies over which they have direct control.

Authorities should increase public sector hiring of young people. Though the public sector is one area of increasing employment, the youth share has declined. Authorities should do what is necessary – setting employment targets and considering job restructuring, if needed – to reverse this trend.

The Commonwealth Employment Service must take a leadership role in placing girls and young women in traditionally male jobs; this should include setting performance targets. As the most important labour market intermediary, the CES is in a unique position to exert leverage on behalf of girls and young women in assuring that they get a fair share of "traditionally male jobs".

Authorities should set performance targets for the Commonwealth Employment Service with respect to placing young people in jobs. Young people lacking experience and skills are in a weak competitive position in the labour market and need preferential treatment to offset the evident bias against them.

CES should refer young people to part-time employment only when such employment is necessary to allow a young person to continue in education or training activities, and when such employment is adequately protected. The CES should not, as a matter of public policy, support part-time employment for young people.

ii) *Introduce structural changes to increase overall employment;* working time and wages are two variables that might be adjusted so as to improve overall employment, and thereby improve prospects for young people

In the short and medium term, Australian authorities should consider the experience of other countries in reducing working time as a way to increase employment. A number of countries are considering or have adopted policies intended to generate employment by reducing work time through early retirement and shorter work weeks. The record of these strategies with respect to cost and net job creation impact is indeterminate so far. Authorities should monitor the experience of other countries for the purpose of determining whether reduced working time schemes could be adapted to Australian needs.

In the longer term, Australian authorities are likely to have no choice but to encourage reduced working time. There is a risk that the increased use of high technology is almost certain to displace labour. Unless Australian authorities develop policies to spread work through a shorter work day and, perhaps, shorter total working time, Australian society may find itself divided into a shrinking productive population supporting a growing, non-working leisure class.

Australian authorities should not reduce youth award wages as a way of increasing youth employment. A reduction in youth wages relative to adult wages risks displacing low-wage adults. Moreover, it is not at all clear from research in Australia or elsewhere how much a reduction in youth wages would increase youth employment.

Authorities should support further development of labour market information, particularly forecasts of manpower and skill requirements at the local labour market level. This kind of information will improve operations of labour markets in the long run by giving education and training planners more of the information they need to assure that their courses of study are relevant to labour market conditions. It will also help young people in choosing careers and planning education and training activities.

iii) *Create jobs for young people*

Regardless of the effectiveness of macro-economic and labour market management policies, job creation will be needed to help cancel the job deficit.

Australian authorities should continue to support job-creation programmes such as the Community Employment Programme, reserving those jobs for the most disadvantaged youths and the long-term unemployed. Job creation is expensive and its long-term value for persons once they leave a job is marginal. It should be reserved as a last resort for those young people least equipped to compete in the labour market and requiring long-term educational and training assistance before they will be able to compete.

Subsidised employment should provide, as much as possible, training and access to informal networks. The value of subsidised jobs can be increased if they provide some training and if, by their proximity to internal labour markets or more regular employment, they provide access to and information about more permanent job prospects.

Australian authorities should encourage development of local employment initiatives. Small businesses are an important source of employment growth. Encouraging small, locally-based, employee-directed co-operatives and other ventures producing social goods offers promise for increasing employment at no or relatively low net costs.

An Entitlement to Orchestrate Opportunities

Presently, the existing education and training arrangements for young people are too uneven in their quality and quantity, and too loosely connected to assure that all young people are prepared for employment or informed to make decisions regarding education, training and work.

Authorities should establish a Youth Entitlement for those young people continuing education or training beyond the compulsory level, and an Entitlement Year for those who leave upon completion of compulsory schooling to assure that all young people have the opportunity to receive adequate preparation for work and adulthood. The Youth Entitlement should guarantee that all young people continuing education beyond the compulsory level or entering training are clearly advised about their choices, can make an easy transition across institutional lines (from secondary school to TAFE or apprenticeship, for example), and will receive job search, career planning and life skills training and an orientation to the world of work, regardless of the particular course of study they pursue in education or training.

The Entitlement Year should guarantee that those young people who do not continue in upper secondary education, enroll in TAFE or enter apprenticeship training, are not left to fend for themselves with regard to preparing for adulthood and work. The Entitlement Year should guarantee the opportunity for job search, career planning and life skills training and orientation to the world of work, and a certificate reflecting basic work-readiness competences, as well as eligibility for income support.

Establishing Responsibility for Youth Policies

Though the Commonwealth is attempting to develop a "youth policy" for Australia, such a policy (or set of policies) requires co-operation and participation not just by the Commonwealth but by state and local governments, unions, employers and young people. The respective roles of all the actors cannot be directed centrally but must be established through negotiation and consensus-building in the process of developing, implementing and managing various interventions. The Commonwealth, sensibly, has taken the leadership in this process, but in order for it to work, its role needs to be a restrained one. Specifically:

Australia's "youth policies" should not be developed as Commonwealth policy but as a national policy. The Commonwealth lacks authority over major elements of what is required for comprehensive policies serving young people.

Policy development must encourage the flow of information and ideas not just to the Commonwealth but to the other players as well. Because the responsibility for the policies affecting youth are scattered among various actors, it is impossible to use a centralised approach in designing policies. The Commonwealth should assure that those with responsibility get the information they need to make informed changes in their policies, and to assure that their policies are consistent and compatible with the policies of other actors.

The Commonwealth should use its central position to provide certain kinds of support and technical assistance to other actors responsible for particular aspects of youth policies. In particular, the Commonwealth can provide advice on various activities to increase female enrolments in "non-traditional" courses of study and training, innovations in secondary curriculum and instructional techniques, and standards for evaluating academic and occupational skill competences.

The Commonwealth should delegate management of federal programmes (such as employment programmes) to a level as close to the client contact level as possible, and encourage similar delegation of authority by the state. In this respect, the Commonwealth should continue the decentralisation it has carried on under the Community Employment Programme and the Participation and Equity Programme. It should also provide assistance to local government and community organisations to help build the necessary management capacity.

Evaluation of youth policies should be linked ultimately to changes in education and training attainment and labour force experience. This will require more information from education and training institutions as well as time-series data on (samples of) individual young persons. Without that information, authorities have little basis for judging the results of various interventions.

Determining Resource Levels

In making their analysis and recommendations, the examiners have not tried to keep the cost of what they propose at the same level as what is spent now on young people. There are two reasons for this:

i) On the basis of public expenditures and tax effort in other OECD countries, it appears to the examiners that Australia can afford to pay more for young people;

ii) The notion of trying to hold costs to (or close to) current spending levels is based on an artificially narrow concept of costs. If authorities do indeed want to hold costs constant they should at least take into account total net costs to government and society, not just budget costs to the Commonwealth in the next fiscal year, for example. This means that authorities need to be aware of long-term government costs of alternatives (costs such as long-term income support costs and prison costs) and social costs (unemployment, social unrest and criminal activity).

BIBLIOGRAPHY

Arbejdsdirectoratet, *The Equal Employment Opportunity Work of the Danish Public Employment Service* (mimeo) 1982.

Australian Confederation of Trade Unions, "ACTU Submission to the OECD Review of Youth Policies, Programmes and Issues", 25 November 1983.

Australian Council of State School Organisations, Inc., "Participation – For What?", prepared for presentation to the visiting OECD examiners on 1 December 1983.

Australian Council of Trade Unions, *Consolidation of ACTU Policy Decisions, 1951-1982.*

Beare, Hedley and Gerald Burke, "Some Economic Aspects of School Building Construction in Australia", (mimeo) OECD, Paris: July 1983.

Budget Statements: 1983-84, circulated by Hon. P.J. Keating, MP and Hon. J.P. Dawkins, MP. Australian Government Publishing Service, Canberra: 1983.

Programme Presentation of Appropriations and Outlays – Department Estimates: 1983-84, presented by Hon. J.P. Dawkins, MP. Australian Government Publishing Service, Canberra: 1983.

Bureau of Labour Market Research, *Employment and Training Programmes for Young People: Analysis of Assistance in 1980-81.* Australian Government Publishing Service, Canberra: 1983.

Bureau of Labour Market Research, *Youth Wages, Employment and the Labour Force.* Australian Government Publishing Service, Canberra: 1983.

CEDEFOP, *Descriptions of the Vocational Training Systems: Denmark.* European Centre for the Development of Vocational Training, Berlin: 1977.

Central Council of Education, *U90: Danish Educational Planning and Policy in a Social Context at the End of the 20th Century.* Danish Ministry of Education, Copenhagen: 1978.

Commission of the European Communities, *Comparative Tables of the Social Security Schemes in the Member States of the European Communities: 12th Edition (Situation at 1 July 1982).* Office for the Office Publications of the European Communities, Luxembourg: 1982.

"Commitment to the Community", in *The Educational Magazine,* Volume 39, No. 5, 1982.

Committee of Inquiry into Education and Training, *Education, Training and Employment,* Volumes I and II. Australian Government Publishing Service, Canberra: 1979;
"Report on follow-up during 1980 of the Report of the Committee of Inquiry into Education and Training (Williams Committee)". Issued by the Ministers for Education and Employment and Industrial Relations, Canberra: 1981;
"Report on follow-up during 1981 issued by the Ministers for Education and Employment and Youth Affairs", Canberra, 1982.

Commonwealth Employment Service, *Job Guide for Western Australia: 1983.* Australian Government Publishing Service, Canberra: 1983.

Commonwealth-State Apprenticeship Committee, *Essential Features of Australian Apprenticeship Systems.* Australian Government Publishing Service, Canberra: 1983.

Commonwealth Tertiary Education Commission, *Learning and Earning: A Study of Education and Employment Opportunities for Young People,* Volumes 1 and 2. Australian Government Publishing Service, Canberra: 1982.

Community Youth Support Scheme, "Guideline Recommendations from the National Consultative Body", Adelaide; 23 November 1981.

Community Youth Support Scheme, "Policy Statement from the National Consultative Body for the Triennium: 1981/82-1983/84", Adelaide; 23 November 1981.

Confederation of Australian Industry Industrial Council, *The Training of Skilled Tradesmen in Australia,* February 1982.

Confederation of Australian Industry National Employers' Industrial Council on Education, *Education and Training in Australia,* August 1978.

Council for Science and Society, *New Technology: Society, Employment and Skill,* Report of a Working Party. The Council for Science and Society, London: 1981.

Department of Education and Youth Affairs, *A Guide to the Commonwealth Government's Programmes and Services for Young People.* Australian Government Publishing Service, Canberra: 1983.

Department of Employment and Youth Affairs, *Report of the Task Force on the Review of Guidelines for the Community Youth Support Scheme.* Australian Government Publishing Service, Canberra: 1982.

Department of Employment and Industrial Relations, *Annual Report 1982-1983.* Australian Government Publishing Service, Canberra: 1983.

Department of Employment and Industrial Relations, Women's Bureau, *Facts on Women in Australia: 1982.* Australian Government Publishing Service, Canberra: 1983.

Department of Employment and Industrial Relations, Women's Bureau, *Gender Wage Differentials in Australia.* DEIR, Canberra: 1983.

Department of Social Security, *Annual Report: 1982-83.* Australian Government Publishing Service, Canberra: 1983.

Department of Social Security, Social Welfare Policy Secretariat, *Report on Poverty Measurement.* Australian Government Publishing Service, Canberra: 1981.

Ewen, John, *Youth in Australia – A New Deal and a New Role.* Phillip Institute of Technology, Melbourne, Victoria: 1983.

Farkas, George, et al., *Impacts from the Youth Incentive Entitlement Pilot Projects.* Abt Associates, Cambridge, MA: December 1982.

"The Fight for the Right to Work", interview with Anna-Greta Leijon, *Sweden Now,* February 1984.

Fisher, N. and P. Scherer, *Research on Commonwealth Employment and Training Programmes and Services.* Bureau of Labour Market Research, Canberra: 1983.

Ford, G.W, "Human Resource Development in Australia and the Balance of Skills", in *Journal of Industrial Relations,* September 1982.

Hayes, Christopher, et al., *Training for Skill Ownership: Learning to Take It with You.* Institute of Manpower Studies, Brighton: 1983.

Hewton, M.P., "Towards the Transfer of Education Buildings to the Local Community – The Elizabeth Experience", prepared for an OECD Conference on Provision and Management of School Buildings.

Holmes, G.A., "The Cost of a Youth Guarantee in the Ballarat Region", prepared for Community Action for Youth, Ballarat College of Advanced Education.

Howard, Michael, "Poverty Lines in the 1980s: Rejection or Redevelopment", in *Social Security Journal,* December 1982.

Industrial and Commercial Training Commission (South Australia), *1982/83 Annual Report,* 1983.

Kuenstler, Peter, "Local Employment Industries in Western Europe", in *International Labour Review,* Vol. 123, No. 2, March-April 1984.

Merrilees, W.J., *Apprenticeship/Training and the Teenage Labour Market.* Bureau of Labour Market Research, Canberra: 1983.

Merrilees, W.J., "Towards An Integrated System of Vocational Training Programmes: The Youth Guarantee Concept", in *The Journal of Industrial Relations,* December 1983.

Minister of Education for Victoria, *Ministerial Review of Post-compulsory Schooling: Discussion Pages,* Melbourne, April 1984.

The Nationwide Workers with Youth Forum, "Recommendations from the National Conference", Sydney, November 1983.

New South Wales Division of Vocational Guidance Services, Department of Industrial Relations, *Background to Careers: 1982.* NSW Department of Industrial Relations, East Sydney: 1982.

OECD, *Australia": Transition from School to Work,* Paris: 1977.

OECD, "The Competences Needed in Working Life", Paris: 1982 (document for general distribution).

OECD, *Compulsory Schooling in a Changing World,* Paris: 1983.

OECD, *Economic Surveys 1982-83: Australia*, Paris: 1983.

OECD/CERI, *Education and Work: The Views of the Young*, Paris: 1983.

OECD, *Educational Policy and Planning: Transition from School to Work or Further Study in Australia*, Paris: 1976.

OECD, *The Industrial Policy of Australia*, Paris: 1975.

OECD, *Manpower Policy in Australia*, Paris: 1975.

OECD, *Public Expenditure on Income Maintenance Programmes*, Paris: 1976.

OECD, *Review of Student Support Schemes in Selected OECD Countries*, Paris: 1978.

OECD/CERI, "Towards a Guarantee of Youth Opportunities" Paris: 1984 (document for general distribution).

OECD, *Youth without Work: Three Countries Approach the Problem*, Paris: 1981.

OECD, *Youth Unemployment*, Vol. I and II, Paris: 1978.

OECD, *Youth Unemployment: The Causes and Consequences*, Paris: 1980.

OECD, *The Welfare State in Crisis*, Paris: 1981.

Paterson, P.R., K.R. MacKay, *Working Paper No. 11, Changes in the Youth Labour Market: 1971 to 1981*. Bureau of Labour Market Research, Canberra: October 1982.

Phillip Institute of Technology, Seminar on the Shears/Mathews Report: "Youth Policies", 28 July 1983.

Pitman, David, *The Determination of Junior Wages in Australia: Needs, Work Value and Employment*. Bureau of Labour Market Research, Canberra: 1983.

"Preliminary Note on Experiments with a Youth Guarantee Scheme: 22 November 1979". Ministry of Labour, Ministry of Education; Denmark: 1980.

Roberts, Pamela and Andrew Herscovitch, "History of Australian Social Security", in *Social Security Journal*, December 1980.

Saunders, Peter, *Equity and Impact on Families of the Australian Tax-Transfer System*. Institute of Family Studies, Melbourne: 1982.

Saunders, Peter, "Evidence on Income Redistribution by Governments" in OECD Economics and Statistics Department *Working Papers*. OECD, Paris: January 1984.

Schools Commission *Schooling for 15 and 16 Year-olds*. Schools Commission, Canberra: 1982.

Sharp, Cathie and Barbara Pocock, *Hunter Equal Opportunity Programme* (mimeo) August 1982.

Shears, L.W. and J.K. Mathews, *Youth Policies: A Report to the Hon. Robert Fordham, MP, Minister of Education*. Office of the Co-ordinator General of Education, Victoria: 1983.

Smith, Ralph, "Sorting out Responsibilities for Training the Work Force", in *Centre for Economic Policy Research Discussion Papers*. Australian National University, Canberra: May 1983.

South Australian Youth Forum, "Say-So". Youth Bureau, Department of Labour South Australia; Adelaide: March 1983.

Stretton, Alan, *Working Paper No. 15, The Short Term Impact of Participants of Selected Youth Employment and Training Programmes*. Bureau of Labour Market Research, Canberra: November 1982.

Subcommittee on Human Services Programmes, *Human Services Programmes Report: Main Report*, Melbourne: 1983.

Tertiary Education Authority of South Australia, "Information Paper for OECD Conference", Adelaide: 30 November 1983.

United States Department of Health and Human Services, *Social Security Programs throughout the World: 1981 (Revised: 1982)*. United States Government Printing Office, Washington, D.C.: 1982.

Willis, the Hon. Ralph, "Department of Employment and Industrial Relations Programmes 1983-84". DEIR, Canberra: August 1983.

Youth Affairs Council of Australia, *Creating Tomorrow Today*. Youth Affairs Council of Australia, July 1983.

Victoria Ethnic Affairs Commission, Division of Research and Policy, *Migrants and the Workforce: Unemployment Trends*. Victorian Ethnic Affairs Commission, Melbourne: 1983.

Zervos, Komninos K., *Australian Greek Welfare Society, Youth Policy*, May 1983.

Part Two

RECORD OF THE REVIEW MEETING
Paris, 28th March 1985

RECORD OF THE REVIEW MEETING

At the 63rd Session of the Manpower and Social Affairs Committee 27th-29th March 1985, one day was devoted to a special High-level Review Meeting on Youth Policies in Australia. This meeting was chaired by Mr. Almunia, Minister of Labour for Spain. Several countries had sent special delegations. The examiners presented the foregoing report and the Australian delegation, led by Mr. Dawkins, Minister for Trade and Minister Assisting the Prime Minister in Youth Affairs, and assisted by Mr. Abrahart, Office of Youth Affairs, responded to the issues raised both by the examiners and members of other national delegations.

Mr. Almunia pointed out that the meeting was important because the OECD countries faced high unemployment among young people as well as among adults. He noted that the problem was a long-term structural one that defied quick solutions, but needed to be addressed or we would lose a generation of young people. He noted the importance of education and training in improving the qualifications of young people for work and the need for policies to create employment. He questioned how much flexibility in labour markets would prepare young people for future employment, if such flexibility contributed to part-time, low-skill jobs. He also suggested that any public policies for young persons had to stress co-operation between the public and private sectors, because public-sector employment alone was no solution.

Mrs. Bjerregaard in her opening remarks stressed the general view of the examiners about the overriding importance of increasing and improving education and training in Australia. She underlined the importance of introducing an Entitlement to provide the impetus for the necessary changes and improvements in the education area. She also stressed that the Commonwealth needed to take a strong leadership role by its example and action to improve the experience of females in labour market, education, training and income support programmes.

Mr. Dawkins noted that since the time at which the review had been done, responsibility for youth affairs had been moved to the Prime Minister's Department to provide better leadership across all the government agencies that might be involved in serving young people. He noted that the OECD report, together with another report on employment programmes (the Kirby Report), was providing valuable input for decisions that the Australian government was taking this year and added that the OECD report was not "just another report" and was indeed being viewed as the basis for planning specific measures. He also added that it was particularly appropriate that the two reports were available for discussion to guide action during the International Youth Year.

Mr. Dawkins also noted that when the current government came to power in early 1983, youth unemployment was peaking and had declined significantly since then. That improvement was attributed to an overall improvement in the Australian economy. There had also been recent improvements in education and training enrolments, improvements that were especially welcome in light of Australia's low education and training participation, and the examiners' heavy emphasis on these areas. He noted that the government was increasing the number of places available in tertiary education. However, Mr. Dawkins said that authorities decided that, in light of the impact of income support on participation in education and training, they would overhaul income support before making more sweeping changes in other arrangements. In that regard, he noted that his authorities were proposing changes in income support provisions along the lines of those suggested in the examiners' report, though such changes were not finalised.

Mr. Dawkins concluded that in trying to improve opportunities for young people, his authorities were not looking for a grand strategy, but were trying to adjust policies across a range of areas. He also noted that the situation of young women was a central consideration in the proposals that were being considered.

The meeting was broken into four themes.

Theme 1: An Entitlement and Alternative Employment Opportunities for Young People

In introducing this theme, *Mrs. Bjerregaard* stressed the importance of arranging institutional structures so as to help young people make better informed decisions about education and training, and to help them better to execute those decisions. Mrs. Bjerregaard suggested that in establishing objectives, authorities needed to recognise that, as the Manpower and Social Affairs Committee concluded in 1983, the customary transition from school to work was fast becoming a myth and that new initiatives should reflect that new reality. This meant that new initiatives, rather than simply adding on to existing structures, had to, among other things, contribute to fundamental changes in mainstream institutions. She also stressed the importance of thinking about changes in arrangements that went beyond the changes in income support schemes which, in the examiners' opinion, distracted from important institutional changes. Mrs. Bjerregaard then posed the first three questions:

Question 1: Are the Australian authorities establishing a youth "Entitlement" or "guarantee"? If so, what are its goals and what are the major features of this scheme for achieving those goals?

Question 2: How will responsibility for developing and implementing a coherent set of youth policies (such as an Entitlement or guarantee) be divided among the Commonwealth, state and local governments? How will the Commonwealth ensure that its state and local partners participate?

Question 3: How feasible would it be to expand employment opportunities for young people using local initiatives and other community-based co-operative ventures?

Mr. Dawkins prefaced his response with the comment that in the federal system in Australia, it was difficult for the government to ensure the kind of coordination that was needed. To cope with this difficulty, the Commonwealth had convened regular meetings of state Youth Affairs Ministers.

One approach to the development of an Entitlement was suggested in the Kirby Report on labour market programmes, which recommended establishing an Australian youth service to coordinate both existing and new services for young people. Regardless of whether such a service was established, the Commonwealth was trying to coordinate existing programmes in a way to provide better counselling and preparation, and income support to encourage participating in education and training. Such an arrangement might not look exactly like the Entitlement proposed by the examiners, but it would serve the same end. The Commonwealth had also endorsed the establishment of traineeships that would combine work and training in a system similar to, but separate from, apprenticeship.

Mr. Abrahart of the Australian delegation elaborated on Mr. Dawkins comments, adding that the traineeships would focus on 16-17 year-old early school-leavers. Additionally, the Commonwealth was pursuing strategies to add youth services and additional education and training places that would help reduce and eventually eliminate youth unemployment. While shying away from providing a legal guarantee, the Australian authorities did accept the objectives suggested in the examiners' report. Mr. Abrahart also noted that the Commonwealth had announced two programmes to help in the development of local employment initiatives that might increase the number of jobs for young people. The Australian authorities were hoping that one of the programmes, a training programme, would reduce the high failure rate experienced by such initiatives in other countries. The other programme, a funding programme which would start on a small scale, would be based on continuing income support at a level roughly equivalent to unemployment benefits.

Sir Richard O'Brien welcomed the action that the Australian authorities had taken. He noted that it was in part because of the difficulties of a federal system that the examiners had recommended a guarantee or Entitlement. The examiners suggested an Entitlement as a way of focusing attention of the states, the Commonwealth departments in Canberra, the employers and unions on the problems of young people and on producing results for their benefit. He added that, in identifying a well-specified set of outcomes, the Entitlement proposed by the examiners would provide the basis for monitoring results, regardless of who was responsible for particular services and activities.

Mr. Dawkins recognised the importance of providing a focus on youth. However, he suggested that the Commonwealth was taking a different approach to accomplish the same end. In doing this they hoped to avoid raising expectations about an Entitlement before the pieces for delivering the required services were in place. Mr. Dawkins noted that Australia already had a guarantee of sorts by which school-leavers who failed to find jobs or enter full-time education were entitled to unemployment benefit. The hope of the Australians was to guarantee more opportunities, such as more education and training places. But they were hesitant to propose a legal guarantee before the capacity was there to provide it.

Mrs. Fuchs acknowledged the difficulty of delivering services through a decentralised federal system, and at the same time guaranteeing certain outcomes or opportunities. However, she noted that the examiners blamed the high unemployment among early school-leavers on the absence of a structured system for preparation for work. She suggested a need for more structure to the system of vocational preparation for young people, backed up by public authorities and the social partners. She emphasized the importance of providing more than money, of guaranteeing realistic preparation for work. Moreover, the guarantee should not be preparation just for immediate employment, but for the long-term skill requirements of the labour market.

Mrs. Bjerregaard, preferring the examiners' concept of an Entitlement, added that their objective was to create an obligation for the authorities to take care that no young person left school without any preparation for work. She also said that the examiners' emphasis on the Entitlement concept was to broaden the debate on a "guarantee" beyond income support arrangements and to create an obligation for the authorities to make institutional changes as well, and to orchestrate opportunities.

In the general discussions, it was suggested that a youth guarantee should not be seen as a new and separate measure, but as a way of rationalising and better structuring existing arrangements to improve utilisation of normal educational arrangements and the normal labour market services, though at-risk youth might need certain extra measures. It was also suggested that both political and administrative mechanisms were needed to ensure coordination.

One delegate to the Manpower and Social Affairs Committee also questioned whether the Australian authorities could delegate more labour market functions from the federal level to the state level, the level at which education decisions were made. *Mr. Dawkins* indicated that the Commonwealth was in fact able to influence state education decisions by creating new programmes that were administered jointly by state and Commonwealth authorities. However, he also noted that delegating responsibility for labour market programmes to the state level would also mean reversing a decision made after World War II and delegating responsibility for the employment service back to the states. He suggested that that could contribute to a breakdown in the uniformity of employment service functions.

In the course of general discussion, members of the Manpower and Social Affairs Committee expressed reservations about relying on subsidised jobs and local labour initiatives. They questioned the value of such employment in improving the long-term employability of young people in "the open labour market", and suggested that subsidised employment, at a minimum, be combined with training. Though there was support for including such employment alternatives in the arsenal of youth measures, Committee members agreed with the examiners that such measures were likely to have only marginal impacts on the employment prospects for young people.

In concluding the discussion on Theme I, Mr. Dawkins responded to another question, saying that the Australian authorities were sensitive to the danger of overcompensating for young people at the expense of others. But he noted that the relatively recent deterioration in the youth labour market required some extraordinary measures. He indicated that without a healthy macro-economic climate, there would be little improvement for young people. However, even with such improvements as were underway now, further selective measures were needed.

Mr. Dawkins said his authorities were trying to provide a trampoline, that would not just catch young unemployed people, but bounce them back into the economic mainstream with the preparation they needed. To do this, the Australians were improving selective measures and then bringing them together in a visible and accessible system that would be locally controlled and managed. His authorities had not yet decided on how much compulsion there would be in making eligibility for income support contingent on participation in education or training, nor had they decided on how benefits would be targeted.

Theme II: Employment and Unemployment

Sir Richard O'Brien introduced Theme II. He welcomed the improvements in the Australian economy and overall employment prospects and noted the success of certain employment initiatives and short-term measures to relieve the youth unemployment crisis. However, he warned against becoming preoccupied with these short-term measures while forgetting longer-term needs. Sir Richard noted that labour markets in Australia, as elsewhere, are moving in directions that were hurting young people. The number of opportunities for them were shrinking because of changes in the structure of work. This raised the prospect of high youth unemployment even in a healthy economy. The dramatic increase in part-time employment was the best indication of this. These jobs were worrisome not only as a signal of changing opportunities, but because they, in themselves, were less valuable in preparing young people for later work.

Question 4: Presuming that the experience of young people in the labour market is a reflection of a larger problem of general unemployment (with the same causes at its roots) and a product of a set of structural factors that put youth at a particular disadvantage relative to others, what can you do for the young?

Question 5: Why has there been an increase in part-time and a decline in full-time employment for young people? What is happening on the supply side (are young people mixing part-time employment with education?) and on the demand side (fewer full-time jobs available for young people?)

Question 6: Do the Australian authorities want to postpone systematically full-time employment for young people?

Mr. Dawkins accepted the importance of macro-economic conditions as one important determinant of employment prospects for young people. He noted that the decline in employment for young people was due in large part to declines in certain sectors. In response to that, the Australian authorities were taking steps to revitalise certain sectors where young people had worked before. But since that revitalisation would mean changing skill requirements, the Australian authorities welcomed and agreed with the examiners' emphasis on improving education and training arrangements to equip young people better for work.

Mr. Dawkins noted that, though under the centralised wage-setting system governing full-time employment real-wage costs were currently declining, the system did have rigidities which were contributing to more part-time employment, especially for young people. While the Australian authorities preferred full-time to part-time employment, they were not resisting part-time employment because it had permitted jobs that might not otherwise exist. Additionally the Commonwealth was supporting employment programmes targeted on the most disadvantaged. Though improved economic circumstances might reduce the need for such programmes, the Australian authorities considered them essential for those who could not find unsubsidised employment.

Mr. Dawkins said that his authorities were not trying to postpone full-time employment for young people, but were rather trying to postpone their withdrawal from the education system. Their first objective was to bring retention in education and training to levels more in line with those in other OECD countries. If this postponed the entry of young people into the workforce, that was acceptable, if it meant that they were better prepared for work.

Mr. Abrahart pointed out the dramatic increase in part-time employment and attributed it to both structural changes favouring the service sector of the economy in which part-time employment was more common, and to an increase in women and students entering the workforce, but not interested in full-time jobs. He also indicated that because allowances to students were set at levels below unemployment benefits, there were greater incentives for students to look for extra sources of income. *Mrs. Fuchs* noted that part-time employment for students was acceptable. But she argued that there was a danger of viewing part-time employment as a substitute for a full-time job, and as a solution to unemployment. One of the dangers of such part-time work was that it was not protected the way full-time jobs were, and did not provide for a transition to stable, full-time jobs. Moreover, there was evidence that young people and women were treated differently from adult males in part-time employment. She added that if there was really a great need for part-time employment, the best way to have it was to reduce working hours across the board.

Sir Richard O'Brien responding to a comment by a Committee member about the negative effect of high youth wages on the number of jobs for young people, called attention to the fact that the evidence on the role of youth wages as a factor in youth unemployment in Australia was ambiguous, and that reducing youth wages was not likely to yield much increase in youth employment. He also recalled the earlier observation by Mr. Dawkins that the Australian authorities did not consider reductions in wages for young people as a useful tool for improving their situation. *Mr. Abrahart* also elaborated on the Australian view of the importance of youth wages. While agreeing that evidence showed that a reduction in youth wages would increase youth employment, he added that the relationship did not appear to be sufficiently strong to warrant reducing youth wages as a way of increasing youth employment. He added that the Australians accepted the view of the examiners that, to the extent youth did have lower productivity, the appropriate policy response was to undertake training to raise productivity, not to reduce youth wages.

Theme III: Education and Training.

Mrs. Fuchs introduced Theme III, noting that though youth unemployment was an immediate crisis, the examiners felt that the most pressing need was for increased educational attainment and skill competences. There were four aspects of the current arrangements that were of special concern to the examiners: the relatively low rate of retention in secondary education, the lack of structured transition to activities following secondary education; the uncertainty over the effectiveness of TAFE education and training, and the low rate of participation of females in education and training activities leading to higher-paying occupations. Though she recognised the pressure on politicians to do something in the short term about youth unemployment, Mrs. Fuchs suggested that they needed to take the leadership in putting long-term developmental needs on the Australian agenda for action, and in involving the social partners in meeting these needs.

Question 7: How do the Australian authorities expect the skill and occupational composition of the economy to change over the next 10-15 years and how will the present education and training arrangements be changed to meet the expected skill requirements of such an economy?

Question 8: What steps are being taken to increase enrolment in years eleven and twelve of secondary education? Are there plans to adapt the upper secondary curricula to accommodate better the needs of students not going on to higher education?

Question 9: What actions are the Australian authorities taking to increase enrolment of girls and young women in science and math-oriented curricula in secondary and tertiary education (including TAFE), and in increasing female participation in apprenticeship? What strategies are being pursued to meet these goals?

Mr. Abrahart pointed out the difficulty of forecasting skill needs, but agreed that with rapid technological and structural change, the Australian authorities saw a need for more flexibility in the training system and for providing broad-based skill training. The traineeships that the Australians planned to launch would expand training capacity significantly. They would also avoid narrow occupation-specific skills. Australian authorities also saw a need to change secondary education in order to increase educational attainment to meet the skill needs not just of high-technology jobs, but to keep pace with rising minimum requirements of lower-skilled jobs as well, and to equip young people with the competences they would need for subsequent vocational training and education. In this regard, the Australian authorities were trying over the longer term to increase secondary retention and improve the linkages between secondary and tertiary education and training. Until now, secondary education had consisted of two paths, one leading to higher education, and the second to other activities. This second path was the one that authorities were working to improve and link better to other education and training opportunities.

Mrs. Bjerregaard asked if the apprenticeship system was being left unchanged and if the proposed traineeships were being created essentially for women. *Mr. Abrahart* pointed out that past attempts to change apprenticeship had failed, and that traineeships offered an opportunity for a new vocational system that would add to apprenticeship (possibly providing a stepping stone to apprenticeship). He said that about 50 per cent of all traineeships would be targeted for girls. Australian authorities had tried to increase female enrolments in apprenticeship. But another way to increase vocational training for girls was to create a new vocational path. In response to a question from the OECD Secretariat whether this meant that as new occupations emerged, structured vocational preparation would be provided under traineeships, rather than apprenticeship, Mr. Abrahart replied that this would probably be the case. *Mrs. Bjerregaard* underlined the importance of that because it meant minimising the risk of creating a first and second-class training system: apprenticeship for boys and traineeships for girls. Speaking more generally, Mrs. Bjerregaard indicated that if females were to have truly equal access in the labour market to what were now male-dominated jobs, they needed to have comparable education and training.

Mr. Dawkins added that his authorities were very much in agreement with the examiners' emphasis on education and training. They were hoping to encourage state education authorities to take action to reach these goals through coaxing and financial incentives. There were a number of initiatives to increase female enrolments in male-dominated courses of study and apprenticeship. Some of this was geared to persuading employers, but much was geared to changing the views of girls and young women as well.

Mrs. Bjerregaard enquired further about the traineeships asking which occupations they would cover, how long they would take, what salary levels there would be, and how girls and young women would be enrolled in them.

Mr. Dawkins said Australian authorities intended to introduce traineeships in areas not covered by apprenticeship, and were negotiating over the balance between training and work, and salary levels. This was, in part, because apprenticeship, despite its earlier usefulness, was not particularly effective for training generally, and in enrolling and training females in particular. *Mr. Abrahart* said that traineeships would last about a year, covering occupations beyond the traditional apprenticeship occupations. Trainees would probably work three to four days a week and be in classroom training one or two days a week. Salary levels would be negotiated under the usual wage-setting procedures. However, unlike current apprenticeship arrangements, trainees would only be paid for the time on the job. In this sense, costs would be shared. Trainees would forego earnings while on training, the government would pay for training, and employers would pay a wage for time spent on the job.

Mrs. Fuchs endorsed use of broad-based training to equip young people not just for their first job, but for subsequent employment. She also emphasized the importance of winning support of employers and unions for whatever new measures were introduced. In that regard, *Mr. Dawkins* noted that a major weakness of current apprenticeship arrangements was the lack of employer support. Mr. Dawkins mentioned other steps to improve opportunities for females including the recent enactment of equal rights legislation and moves by public service administrators to increase opportunities in public employment.

With regard to secondary education, Mr. Dawkins also said that a survey of young people showed that early school-leavers expected more preparation for work than secondary education provided. He noted that retention in secondary education was improving, but could improve more, especially for low-income students, with changes in the income support arrangements. He responded to a question from the Secretariat about whether there were resources for expanding enrolment in TAFE and secondary education, saying that the Australian authorities hoped to move some people now in TAFE – which was filled to capacity – back into secondary education. Generally, he acknowledged the need to expand places in secondary education and TAFE and pointed out the need for states to assume some of the burden of such expansion. However, he added that additional resources would have to be made available.

Mr. Abrahart responded to a question by the OECD Secretariat, about the reasons for low retention in secondary education. He pointed out that secondary retention was rising – in part due to decisions by students to stay in school in the face of current poor job prospects and in order to increase future employment prospects. But he also said that the availability of exit certificates for early-leavers provided a retention incentive for young people who were not going on to higher education. He added that the Commonwealth hoped to raise retention more with a new initiative designed to make improvements such as introducing a new curriculum for students not going on to higher education, revising assessment practices, sharing decision-making among students, parents and teachers, improving teacher preparation, and improving links with post-school activities. He reiterated that most improvements had to be initiated by the state, not Commonwealth, authorities.

Theme IV: Income Support

Invited by Mrs. Bjerregaard to introduce this theme *Mr. Wurzburg*, of the OECD Secretariat, suggested that income support had been the second most controversial issue in Australia, after concern about unemployment. Indeed, as the day's earlier discussion had demonstrated, income support issues pervaded all other themes. Mr. Wurzburg indicated that the examiners' two greatest concerns with the income support systems arrangements were the complexity in which various allowances created mixed and conflicting incentives, and the fact that there was inadequate attention in the overall "system" of income support given to encouraging long-term economic self-sufficiency.

Question 10: What steps have the Australian authorities decided upon to rationalise better the objectives, eligibility criteria, and benefit levels of the various income support provisions for young people?

Mr. Dawkins said that the Australian government was very much in agreement with the examiners' assessment of the inadequacies of and controversy surrounding the present income support arrangements and their suggestions for improvements. Indeed because of the controversy, Mr. Dawkins was reluctant to go into details except to say that the proposed changes were nearly ready to be announced and were in line with what the examiners recommended. Generally, authorities hoped to simplify benefit levels and test eligibility on the basis of parental income (except for independent youths). Authorities were especially concerned about the present arrangements which paid low-income youth more to leave school and be unemployed than to continue in education and training. Mr. Dawkins observed that many of the present imbalances in income support were attributable to the fact that unemployment benefits were first introduced at a time when youth unemployment was very low. Limited employment opportunities had magnified the impact of the programme on the behaviour of young people. He concluded by noting that his authorities were not adverse to requiring young people to engage in certain activities – training, for example – as a condition of eligibility. That issue was being approached cautiously, however, because such a practice would be a politically sensitive departure from past practices.

Mrs. Bjerregaard welcomed the willingness of the Australian authorities to link eligibility for income support benefits to productive activities that would increase their long-term economic self-sufficiency. She also noted that this was related to the initial discussion on entitlement which was focused on the question of how to assure that time spent outside the labour market would be productive and contribute to increased employability.

Annex

EXCERPTS REGARDING THE TERMS OF REFERENCE OF THE OECD REVIEW OF YOUTH POLICIES IN AUSTRALIA

taken from *Youth Policies, Programmes and Issues: An Australian Background Paper* (published by the Australian authorities, Canberra, 1983)

The Preface to the main report sets out in full the examiners' terms of reference. Briefly, our major concern is with the consequences of very high rates of youth unemployment. Since the mid-seventies, these have risen disturbingly and now stand at 18 per cent (in the case of 15-19 year-olds, 23 per cent). We are concerned not only with the economic and budgetary implications of this but also – indeed more so – with the potentially demoralising effect on the young people of the nation. We are conscious that our upper secondary and tertiary education participation rates are not high by some OECD country standards, and we want to know how we can act most effectively to retain more of our older children in school and to attract more of our school-leavers to higher education or training.

We want to know whether some of our existing structures (education systems and institutions, programmes of financial assistance, or government agencies and their functional responsibilities) are aggravating our present problems or contributing to their solution. For example, are our programmes of unemployment benefit and student assistance (conducted by different government departments) inadvertently geared in such a way as to attract young people away from the classrooms and into the unemployment queues? Or is it employment and the wage arising from it that is attractive to young people? Or, again, is the problem in the nature of the education system and the rewards it does or does not offer?

We want to devise policy options that will remedy inequities in existing programmes and provide more and better opportunities for our young people, whether in conventional employment, in education, in training or in alternative modes of living and working.

We want young women to participate equally with young men in benefiting from these opportunities.

Terms of Reference

The OECD examiners are asked to:

i) Review, in the light of international experience, existing Australian government policies and programmes for those aged 15 to 24 years, in education, training, employment and income support; and to deal with major economic and social problems facing young people in Australia;

ii) Suggest, against the background of likely economic circumstances, ways in which the needs of young people can be better met, including alternative policies, programmes and arrangements in education, training, and employment and income support;

iii) In particular, comment on:
  a) The practicability of a comprehensive and integrated approach to support services for young people, as for example through a "youth guarantee", "youth allowance", or one of the various proposals of this kind developed overseas;
  b) The role of income support structures in providing incentives for young people to continue appropriate education and training, and identify any changes that could be made to existing arrangements;
  c) The appropriate level for Australia of full-time education retention and participation rates at the post-compulsory level;
  d) The applicability to the Australian situation of overseas developments in the area of alternative forms of work and of living arrangements for young people, such as youth co-operatives and community service activities;

iv) In fulfilling the terms of reference take into account structural discrimination against young women and suggest possible remedies that are integral to proposals and programmes for young people generally, with a view to achieving equality of outcomes and full participation for young women.

OECD SALES AGENTS
DÉPOSITAIRES DES PUBLICATIONS DE L'OCDE

ARGENTINA – ARGENTINE
Carlos Hirsch S.R.L., Florida 165, 4° Piso (Galería Guemes)
1333 BUENOS AIRES, Tel. 33.1787.2391 y 30.7122

AUSTRALIA – AUSTRALIE
D.A. Book (Aust.) Pty. Ltd.
11-13 Station Street (P.O. Box 163)
MITCHAM, Vic. 3132. Tel. (03) 873 4411

AUSTRIA – AUTRICHE
OECD Publications and Information Center
4 Simrockstrasse 5300 Bonn (Germany). Tel. (0228) 21.60.45
Local Agent/Agent local:
Gerold and Co., Graben 31, WIEN 1. Tel. 52.22.35

BELGIUM – BELGIQUE
Jean De Lannoy, Service Publications OCDE
avenue du Roi 202, B-1060 BRUXELLES. Tel. 02/538.51.69

CANADA
Renouf Publishing Company Limited/
Éditions Renouf Limitée Head Office/Siège social – Store/Magasin:
61, rue Sparks Street,
OTTAWA, Ontario K1P 5A6. Tel. (613)238-8985. 1-800-267-4164
Store/Magasin: 211, rue Yonge Street,
TORONTO, Ontario M5B 1M4. Tel. (416)363-3171
Regional Sales Office/
Bureau des Ventes régional:
7575 Trans-Canada Hwy., Suite 305,
SAINT-LAURENT, Québec H4T 1V6. Tel. (514)335-9274

DENMARK – DANEMARK
Munksgaard Export and Subscription Service
35, Nørre Søgade
DK 1370 KØBENHAVN K. Tel. +45.1.12.85.70

FINLAND – FINLANDE
Akateeminen Kirjakauppa
Keskuskatu 1, 00100 HELSINKI 10. Tel. 65.11.22

FRANCE
OCDE, 2, rue André-Pascal, 75775 PARIS CEDEX 16
Tel. (1) 45.24.82.00
Librairie/Bookshop: 33, rue Octave-Feuillet,
75016 PARIS. Tél. (1) 45.24.81.67 ou (1) 45.24.81.81
Principal correspondant:
13602 AIX-EN-PROVENCE: Librairie de l'Université.
Tél. 42.26.18.08

GERMANY – ALLEMAGNE
OECD Publications and Information Center
4 Simrockstrasse 5300 BONN Tel. (0228) 21.60.45

GREECE – GRÈCE
Librairie Kauffmann, 28 rue du Stade,
ATHÈNES 132. Tel. 322.21.60

HONG-KONG
Government Information Services,
Publications (Sales) Office,
Beaconsfield House, 4/F.,
Queen's Road Central

ICELAND – ISLANDE
Snæbjörn Jónsson and Co., h.f.,
Hafnarstræti 4 and 9, P.O.B. 1131, REYKJAVIK.
Tel. 13133/14281/11936

INDIA – INDE
Oxford Book and Stationery Co.:
NEW DELHI-1, Scindia House. Tel. 45896
CALCUTTA 700016, 17 Park Street. Tel. 240832

INDONESIA – INDONÉSIE
PDIN-LIPI, P.O. Box 3065/JKT., JAKARTA, Tel. 583467

IRELAND – IRLANDE
TDC Publishers – Library Suppliers
12 North Frederick Street, DUBLIN 1 Tel. 744835-749677

ITALY – ITALIE
Libreria Commissionaria Sansoni:
Via Lamarmora 45, 50121 FIRENZE. Tel. 579751/584468
Via Bartolini 29, 20155 MILANO. Tel. 365083
Sub-depositari:
Ugo Tassi
Via A. Farnese 28, 00192 ROMA. Tel. 310590
Editrice e Libreria Herder,
Piazza Montecitorio 120, 00186 ROMA. Tel. 6794628
Agenzia Libraria Pegaso,
Via de Romita 5, 70121 BARI. Tel. 540.105/540.195
Agenzia Libraria Pegaso, Via S. Anna dei Lombardi 16, 80134 NAPOLI.
Tel. 314180.
Libreria Hoepli, Via Hoepli 5, 20121 MILANO. Tel. 865446
Libreria Scientifica, Dott. Lucio de Biasio "Aeiou"
Via Meravigli 16, 20123 MILANO Tel. 807679
Libreria Zanichelli
Piazza Galvani 1/A, 40124 Bologna Tel. 237389
Libreria Lattes, Via Garibaldi 3, 10122 TORINO. Tel. 519274
La diffusione delle edizioni OCSE è inoltre assicurata dalle migliori librerie nelle città più importanti.

JAPAN – JAPON
OECD Publications and Information Center,
Landic Akasaka Bldg., 2-3-4 Akasaka,
Minato-ku, TOKYO 107 Tel. 586.2016

KOREA – CORÉE
Pan Korea Book Corporation,
P.O. Box n° 101 Kwangwhamun, SÉOUL. Tel. 72.7369

LEBANON – LIBAN
Documenta Scientifica/Redico,
Edison Building, Bliss Street, P.O. Box 5641, BEIRUT.
Tel. 354429 – 344425

MALAYSIA – MALAISIE
University of Malaya Co-operative Bookshop Ltd.
P.O. Box 1127, Jalan Pantai Baru
KUALA LUMPUR. Tel. 577701/577072

THE NETHERLANDS – PAYS-BAS
Staatsuitgeverij, Verzendboekhandel,
Chr. Plantijnstraat 1 Postbus 20014
2500 EA S-GRAVENHAGE. Tel. nr. 070.789911
Voor bestellingen: Tel. 070.789208

NEW ZEALAND – NOUVELLE-ZÉLANDE
Publications Section,
Government Printing Office Bookshops:
AUCKLAND: Retail Bookshop: 25 Rutland Street,
Mail Orders: 85 Beach Road, Private Bag C.P.O.
HAMILTON: Retail: Ward Street,
Mail Orders, P.O. Box 857
WELLINGTON: Retail: Mulgrave Street (Head Office),
Cubacade World Trade Centre
Mail Orders: Private Bag
CHRISTCHURCH: Retail: 159 Hereford Street,
Mail Orders: Private Bag
DUNEDIN: Retail: Princes Street
Mail Order: P.O. Box 1104

NORWAY – NORVÈGE
Tanum-Karl Johan a.s
P.O. Box 1177 Sentrum, 0107 OSLO 1. Tel. (02) 80.12.60

PAKISTAN
Mirza Book Agency, 65 Shahrah Quaid-E-Azam, LAHORE 3.
Tel. 66839

PORTUGAL
Livraria Portugal, Rua do Carmo 70-74,
1117 LISBOA CODEX. Tel. 360582/3

SINGAPORE – SINGAPOUR
Information Publications Pte Ltd,
Pei-Fu Industrial Building,
24 New Industrial Road N° 02-06
SINGAPORE 1953, Tel. 2831786, 2831798

SPAIN – ESPAGNE
Mundi-Prensa Libros, S.A.
Castelló 37, Apartado 1223, MADRID-28001, Tel. 431.33.99
Libreria Bosch, Ronda Universidad 11, BARCELONA 7.
Tel. 317.53.08, 317.53.58

SWEDEN – SUÈDE
AB CE Fritzes Kungl Hovbokhandel,
Box 16 356, S 103 27 STH, Regeringsgatan 12,
DS STOCKHOLM. Tel. 08/23.89.00
Subscription Agency/Abonnements:
Wennergren-Williams AB,
Box 30004, 0104 25 STOCKHOLM. Tel. 08/54.12.00

SWITZERLAND – SUISSE
OECD Publications and Information Center
4 Simrockstrasse 5300 BONN (Germany). Tel. (0228) 21.60.45
Local Agents/Agents locaux
Librairie Payot, 6 rue Grenus, 1211 GENÈVE 11. Tel. 022.31.89.50

TAIWAN – FORMOSE
Good Faith Worldwide Int'l Co., Ltd.
9th floor, No. 118, Sec. 2,
Chung Hsiao E. Road. TAIPEI. Tel. 391.7396/391.7397

THAILAND – THAILANDE
Suksit Siam Co., Ltd., 1715 Rama IV Rd,
Samyan, BANGKOK 5. Tel. 2511630

TURKEY – TURQUIE
Kültur Yayinlari Is-Türk Ltd. Sti.
Atatürk Bulvari No: 191/Kat: 21
Kavaklidere/ANKARA. Tel. 17 02 66
Dolmabahce Cad. No: 29
BESIKTAS/ISTANBUL. Tel. 60 71 88

UNITED KINGDOM – ROYAUME-UNI
H.M. Stationery Office,
P.O.B. 276, LONDON SW8 5DT.
(postal orders only)
Telephone orders: (01) 622.3316, or
49 High Holborn, LONDON WC1V 6 HB (personal callers)
Branches at: EDINBURGH, BIRMINGHAM, BRISTOL,
MANCHESTER, BELFAST.

UNITED STATES OF AMERICA – ÉTATS-UNIS
OECD Publications and Information Center, Suite 1207,
1750 Pennsylvania Ave., N.W. WASHINGTON, D.C.20006 – 4582
Tel. (202) 724.1857

VENEZUELA
Libreria del Este, Avda. F. Miranda 52, Edificio Galipan,
CARACAS 106. Tel. 32.23.01/33.26.04/31.58.38

YUGOSLAVIA – YOUGOSLAVIE
Jugoslovenska Knjiga, Knez Mihajlova 2, P.O.B. 36, BEOGRAD.
Tel. 621.992

Les commandes provenant de pays où l'OCDE n'a pas encore désigné de dépositaire peuvent être adressées à:
OCDE, Bureau des Publications, 2, rue André-Pascal, 75775 PARIS CEDEX 16.
Orders and inquiries from countries where sales agents have not yet been appointed may be sent to:
OECD, Publications Office. 2, rue André-Pascal, 75775 PARIS CEDEX 16.

69131-11-1985

OECD PUBLICATIONS, 2, rue André-Pascal, 75775 PARIS CEDEX 16 - No. 43459 1986
PRINTED IN FRANCE
(81 86 01 1) ISBN 92-64-12788-7